QUESTIONS & ANSWERS:
International Law

QUESTIONS & ANSWERS:
International Law

Multiple-Choice and Short-Answer Questions and Answers

REBECCA BRATSPIES
Professor of Law
CUNY School of Law

ISBN: 978-1-4224-1776-8

NOTE TO USERS
To ensure that you are using the latest materials available in this area, please be sure to periodically check the LexisNexis Law School web site for downloadable updates and supplements at www.lexisnexis.com/lawschool.

Editorial Offices
121 Chanlon Rd., New Providence, NJ 07974 (908) 464-6800
201 Mission St., San Francisco, CA 94105-1831 (415) 908-3200
www.lexisnexis.com

MATTHEW◆BENDER

(2011–Pub.3249)

Dedication

For Russ Miller, who got me into this.

About the Author

Rebecca Bratspies is a Professor of Law at CUNY School of Law, where she teaches International Law, Administrative Law, Environmental Law, and International Environmental Law. Professor Bratspies has published widely on issues of environmental regulation, sustainability, and food security. Her recent work explores the problem that uncertainty poses for legal decisionmaking, and the role that law plays in promoting sustainable development. She is also a research scholar with the Center for Progressive Reform in Washington, D.C. She holds a B.A. in Biology from Wesleyan University and a J.D. *cum laude* from the University of Pennsylvania.

Table of Contents

QUESTIONS

1

1. The term International Law refers to:

    (A) Law that governs the relations between states

    (B) Law that governs international organizations

    (C) Law that governs international organizations, the relations between states, and between states and international organizations

    (D) Law that governs international organizations, the relations between states, the relations between states and international organizations, as well as many aspects of state relations with persons (both legal and juridical)

    (E) Law that governs international organizations, the relations between states, the relations between states and international organizations, many aspects of state relations with persons (both legal and juridical), as well as the interactions of sub-national entities with states.

2. The term Transnational Law includes:

    (A) International Law

    (B) Conflict of Laws

    (C) Supranational Law

    (D) Comparative Law

    (E) All of the above

3. The Peace of Westphalia is generally considered to mark:

    (A) The end of World War II and the creation of the United Nations

    (B) The establishment of the modern state and the beginning of international law

    (C) The end of the race among European States for colonies in the New World and the beginning of the decolonization movement

    (D) The end of the Indian Wars and the beginning of westward expansion in the United States

    (E) The end of World War I and the establishment of the League of Nations.

4.   Sovereignty is:

ANSWER:

5.   Under the UN Charter, neither the UN itself, nor its members can take any action that might negatively affect the sovereignty of a state.

(A) TRUE

(B) FALSE

6.   To be a state under international law, an entity must have:

(A) A defined territory

(B) A permanent population

(C) A government

(D) The ability to enter relations with other states

(E) All of the above

7.   A political entity can be a state even if it is not a member of the United Nations.

(A) TRUE

(B) FALSE

8.   Under the declarative theory of statehood, the political existence of states depends on recognition by other states.

(A) TRUE

(B) FALSE

9.   In 1967, three families move onto an abandoned World War II gun platform in the North Sea. The platform is approximately 10 acres in size. The families claim that the platform is *terra nullius*, and declare their intent to form the new country of Sealand. The families develop a flag, issue passports and draft a constitution for their new country. They live on the platform continuously for 40 years. During that time period, no other state recognizes Sealand as a country. Which of the following is most true about Sealand's status under international law?

(A) Sealand cannot be a state under either the declarative or constitutive theories of statehood because it is too small

(B) Sealand might be a state under the declarative theory of statehood but not under the constitutive theory of statehood

    (C) Sealand will only become a state under either the declarative and constitutive theories of statehood if it becomes a member of the United Nations

    (D) Sealand is a state under both the declarative and constitutive theories of statehood because all peoples have the right to self-determination

    (E) Sealand cannot become a state under the declarative or constitutive theories of statehood unless the families obtained control over the platform by conquest

10.   The term "public international law" refers to:

    (A) The law of foreign jurisdictions

    (B) The choice of law to apply when there are conflicts in the domestic law of different states related to private transactions

    (C) The law created by the United Nations

    (D) Then law that governs the relations between states

    (E) The law that governs the conduct of states and of international organizations, as well as some of their relations with persons.

11.   The term "private international law" refers to:

    (A) The law of foreign jurisdictions

    (B) The choice of law to apply when there are conflicts in the domestic law of different states related to private transactions

    (C) The law created by the United Nations

    (D) The law that governs the relations between states

    (E) The law that governs the conduct of states and of international organizations, as well as some of their relations with persons.

12.   To the extent that international law is binding on states, its binding force stems from:

    (A) The power of the International Court of Justice to enforce international laws and commitments

    (B) The police power of the Security Council

    (C) The consent of states

    (D) The police powers of the General Assembly

    (E) All of the above

13.   One significant difference in the institutional structure of international law, when compared

with the institutional structure of national law in that:

(A) International law institutions include a centralized legislature, but not a court of compulsory jurisdiction or an executive with enforcement powers

(B) International law institutions include a centralized legislature and a court of compulsory jurisdiction but not an executive with enforcement power

(C) International law institutions include neither a centralized legislature, a court of compulsory jurisdiction nor an executive with enforcement power

(D) International law institutions include a centralized legislature, a court of compulsory jurisdiction, an executive with enforcement powers and a supra-national Security Council

(E) International law institutions include a centralized legislature, a court of compulsory jurisdiction, an executive with enforcement powers, a supranational Security Council and a General Assembly.

14. Only international courts can decide issues of international law.

(A) TRUE

(B) FALSE

15. Under what two circumstances can a state that is not a party to a treaty nevertheless be bound by the terms of the treaty?

ANSWER:

16. How does international law invoke a state duty of good faith?

ANSWER:

17. The term *lex ferenda* refers to:

(A) Law as it is

(B) Law as it should be

(C) Law as described under the UN Charter

(D) Domestic rather than international law

(E) International rather than domestic law

18. An obligation *erga omnes* is one that:

(A) A state owes to all other states and to the community of states as a whole

(B)   A state commits itself to uphold vis-à-vis other states by virtue of its membership in the United Nations

(C)   An individual owes other individuals under international law

(D)   A state owes its citizens by virtue of signing the United Nations charter

(E)   An individual owes to the state in which s/he resides

19.   Under international law, soft law refers to:

(A)   United Nations treaties that have not yet come into force

(B)   Contracts between private parties and a state that are not binding on non-parties

(C)   Quasi-legal instruments that do not have binding force

(D)   The work of Non-Governmental Organizations

(E)   All of the above

20.   How can soft law become hard law?

ANSWER:

21.   *Jus cogens* norms include:

(A)   Equal pay for equal work

(B)   Prohibitions on piracy, slavery and torture

(C)   One person one vote

(D)   Prohibitions on usury and false witness

(E)   All of the above

22.   A monist theory of international law is one in which:

(A)   All legal authority is derived from international law

(B)   National and international law are viewed as parts of a single system of law

(C)   International law prevails in any conflict between domestic and international law

(D)   Reliance on contrary state domestic law cannot justify violating international law

(E)   All of the above

23.   A dualist theory of international law is one in which:

(A) Domestic and international law are entirely separate legal systems that are viewed as equal in rank.

(B) Breaches of international law are resolved through duels.

(C) Domestic law outranks international law.

(D) A contrary domestic law means that the relevant international law is null and void.

(E) All of the above.

24. International governmental organizations (or IGOs) are:

(A) Associations of private parties that join together to negotiate with states

(B) Associations of private parties that do not enter into treaties or other international agreements

(C) Associations of states established by treaty to pursue the common aims of their member states

(D) Associations of states and private parties that cooperatively manage transboundary resources

(E) All of the above.

25. The European Union and the Council of Europe are examples of similar models for international cooperation.

(A) TRUE

(B) FALSE

26. Under the modern view of international law, the subjects of international law can include:

(A) States

(B) Intergovernmental organizations

(C) Individuals

(D) (A) and (B) only

(E) (A), (B) and (C)

27. Under international law, the principle of self-determination applies to all self-identified peoples and gives them the right to secede and form their own state.

(A) TRUE

(B) FALSE

28. The principle of *uti possidetis*:

    (A) Requires minority groups not to secede from an existing State

    (B) Allows minority groups to secede from an existing State

    (C) Allows newly-independent States to draw their own borders

    (D) Affirms former colonial boundaries as the borders of newly-independent States

    (E) Requires the United Nations to ratify the borders of newly-independent States

29. If a State's government is not recognized by other states (because, for example, it seized power as the result of the violent overthrow of a prior government), the State ceases to exist.

    (A) TRUE

    (B) FALSE

30. If a United States-flagged commercial ship owned by Jon's Shipping Inc. is boarded and seized by Canadian officials while in Canadian territorial waters, what causes of action would exist?

    (A) Only the United States would have an action under international law against Canada for violating the right of innocent passage

    (B) Only Jon's Shipping would have an action under international law against Canada for violating the right of innocent passage

    (C) Both the United States and Jon's Shipping would have an action under international law against Canada for violating the right of innocent passage

    (D) Neither the United States nor Jon's Shipping would have an action under international law against Canada for violating the right of innocent passage because international law does not apply within state territorial waters

    (E) Whether or not the United States and/or Jon's Shipping will have an action under international law will depend on whether Canada's actions are likely to jeopardize international peace and security

31. The phrase "American exceptionalism" refers to:

ANSWER:

32. Which of the following actors would be permitted to bring a contested case before the International Court of Justice?

   (A) Venezuela

   (B) The African Union

   (C) Ulan Bator

   (D) The International Maritime Organization (IMO)

   (E) The Red Cross

33. In conjunction with the non-governmental organization (NGO) Greenpeace, the World Health Organization (WHO) has launched a major international campaign opposing the consumption of genetically-modified foods. As part of this campaign, they are advising states that importing these products infringes on the right to food, thereby violating obligations under the International Covenant on Economic Social and Cultural Rights. As the major producer and exporter of these crops, the United States vehemently opposes this campaign as an intrusion on its national sovereignty, and an unwarranted interference with global trade. In response, the United States is trying to persuade the General Assembly to defund the WHO. The General Assembly is unsure whether the WHO has actually violated international law. Which actor would not be permitted to request an advisory opinion from the ICJ?

   (A) The United States

   (B) Greenpeace

   (C) The WHO (World Health Organization)

   (D) The UN General Assembly

   (E) Both (A) and (B)

34. The International Criminal Court has jurisdiction over:

   (A) Appeals from criminal convictions in national courts, if the national court applied international law

   (B) Multinational corporations accused of human rights abuses in the conduct of their business activities

11

(C) Individuals accused of genocide or other systematic war crimes

(D) Cases of art theft referred by Interpol

(E) All of the above

35. The International Court of Justice automatically has jurisdiction over disputes involving parties to its statute.

(A) TRUE

(B) FALSE

36. What principles must tribunals use in interpreting a treaty obligation?

ANSWER:

37. The International Court of Justice (ICJ):

(A) Has original jurisdiction in all cases arising under international law

(B) Has jurisdiction in cases in accordance with the Statute of the International Court of Justice

(C) Has jurisdiction in any case referred to it by the Security Council

(D) Is the court of final appeal for all cases decided by national courts

(E) All of the above

38. What is the relationship between the International Court of Justice (ICJ) and the Permanent Court of International Justice (PCIJ)?

(A) They are alternative courts, with overlapping jurisdiction

(B) They are parallel courts that divide up international law cases with the ICJ taking public law cases and the PCIJ taking private law cases

(C) The ICJ is the successor court to the PCIJ

(D) The PCIJ is the successor court to the ICJ

(E) As part of the 2005 UN reorganization, the PCIJ was renamed the ICJ

39. The ICJ's jurisdictional competence extends to disputes over:

(A) The interpretation of a treaty

(B) Any question of international law

(C)   The existence of any fact which, if established, would constitute a breach of an international obligation

(D)   The nature or extent of the reparation to be made for the breach of an international obligation

(E)   All of the above

40.   The ICJ has jurisdiction to resolve a contentious case whenever the case:

(A)   Is between state parties that consent to ICJ jurisdiction

(B)   Involves an issue of international law, including treaty interpretation, facts that would establish a breach of international law, or reparations for a breach of international law

(C)   Arose not more than three years before the initial filing of a case before the ICJ

(D)   (A) and (B) only

(E)   (A), (B) and (C)

41.   When a dispute is properly submitted to the ICJ, the ICJ has jurisdiction to resolve:

(A)   The interpretation of a treaty

(B)   Any question of international law

(C)   The existence of any fact which, if established would constitute a breach of an international obligation

(D)   The nature or extent of the reparation to be made for the breach of an international obligation

(E)   All of the above

42.   The ICJ can hear disputes that arise from the actions of the legislature, executive or judicial branches of a state's governments, so long as the challenged actions raise an international law issue that falls within the ICJ's jurisdictional competence.

(A)   TRUE

(B)   FALSE

43.   The United States fails to honor its obligations under the Vienna Convention on Consular Relations to notify foreign citizens held as criminal detainees of their right to contact their embassy for assistance. A detainee who is denied his rights under the Vienna Convention is sentenced to death. The detainee's home state petitions the ICJ for a ruling that the criminal conviction violates the Vienna Convention and must therefore be invalidated. Would the United States be bound by the decision of the ICJ?

(A) Yes, because the Supremacy Clause of the Constitution provides that treaties are the supreme law of the land

(B) No, because the Constitution vests authority to resolve cases and controversies in the Supreme Court

(C) Yes, because the UN Charter, to which the United States is a party, commits the United States to comply with the decisions of the ICJ in any case to which it is a party

(D) No, because it is the President's job to take care that the law be faithfully executed

(E) The answer seems to be "it depends," because the statements (A), (B), (C), and (D) are all true, and may be contradictory

44. What are the primary ways that international law is created?

    (A) Through treaties and the published writings of eminent jurists

    (B) Through international conferences and General Assembly resolutions

    (C) Through agreements and practice

    (D) Through General Assembly and Security Council resolutions

    (E) All of the above

45. Which is not a source of international law?

    (A) Treaties

    (B) International customs and norms

    (C) Conventions

    (D) The United States Constitution

    (E) The writings of eminent scholars and jurists

46. *Opinio Juris* refers to:

    (A) Customary international law

    (B) The opinions expressed by jurists and eminent legal thinkers

    (C) The laws of war

    (D) The members of the International Court of Justice

    (E) (A), (B), and (C)

47. When will a practice be considered customary international law?

    (A) When the practice has become a general practice of states

    (B) When states accept the practice as law

    (C) When the practice has been enshrined in a treaty or convention

(D) When both (A) and (B) are true

(E) When (A), (B), and (C) are true

48. Treaties cannot create customary international law.

(A) TRUE

(B) FALSE

49. Who is bound by a practice considered customary international law?

(A) All states, regardless of their objection

(B) All states, except those that consistently object

(C) Only those states that opt into customary international law

(D) Only those states in existence when the custom is created

(E) All litigants appearing in federal and state court asserting claims under international law

50. An additional source of international law is the general principles of law recognized by civilized nations.

(A) TRUE

(B) FALSE

51. Among the "general principles of law recognized by civilized nations" that have been incorporated into international law are:

(A) Equity

(B) Damages

(C) Trial by jury

(D) (A) and (B) only

(E) All of the above

52. Why does international law incorporate general principles of law?
ANSWER:

53. A treaty is:
ANSWER:

54. A multilateral treaty is:

ANSWER:

55. A treaty can be either a written or an oral agreement.

(A) TRUE

(B) FALSE

56. If the Russian Federation and Defenders of Wildlife (the NGO) enter into an oral agreement concerning protection of endangered species within the Russian Arctic, that agreement is:

(A) A treaty under customary international law

(B) A treaty under the Vienna Convention on the Law of Treaties

(C) An agreement that can never be a treaty and has no legal force under international law

(D) An agreement that would be a treaty if it were reduced to writing and consideration were given

(E) An agreement that would be a treaty if duly ratified by the General Assembly

57. A treaty enters force when:

(A) It is negotiated and signed

(B) When two-thirds of the United Nations membership ratifies the treaty

(C) When the terms for entry into force as specified in the agreement are met

(D) When the members of the United Nations Security Council vote in favor of the treaty

(E) When the United Nations General Assembly adopts the treaty by consensus

58. A reservation to a treaty is:

(A) A unilateral statement made by a State when signing, ratify or acceding to a treaty purporting to exclude or modify the legal effect of certain provisions of the treaty

(B) A unilateral commitment by a State to sign, ratify or accede to a treaty at a specified date in the future

(C) A negotiated commitment by two or more States to modify or otherwise alter their interpretation of a provision of an existing multilateral treaty

(D) A multilateral commitment to negotiate a treaty by a specified date in the future

(E) A political expression of disagreement with a treaty that has no effect on the validity or scope of a treaty

59. If Spain files a reservation to the Framework Convention on Climate Change, a multilateral treaty, that violates the object and purpose of the treaty.

(A) Spain would no longer be a party to the treaty

(B) The treaty is voided

(C) The reservation is valid, but Spain otherwise remains a party to the treaty

(D) The reservation is invalid and Spain remains a party to the treaty

(E) Other parties to the treaty are authorized to use military force under the UN Charter

60. Two or more States may use a reservation to modify, or otherwise alter their interpretation of a provision of an existing multilateral treaty vis-à-vis each other.

(A) TRUE

(B) FALSE

61. A treaty is self-executing when:

(A) It is adopted by two-thirds of the states eligible to ratify it

(B) The language of a treaty specifies that it becomes effective without further legislative action

(C) Congress adopts domestic legislation giving the treaty the force of law

(D) The President declares the treaty will be implemented as the law of the land

(E) It gives individual citizens the right to sue in federal court to enforce the treaty

62. Treaties are agreements between states and therefore can only create state-to-state political obligations, rather than private individual rights.

(A) TRUE

(B) FALSE

63. When a party breaches a multilateral treaty:

(A) The UN Charter authorizes all other parties to the treaty to respond with the use force

(B) The UN Charter authorizes only a party that has been directly affected to respond with the use of force

(C) The entire treaty is voided, and all parties may respond by suspending compliance with the treaty

(D) The particular provision that was violated is voided and all parties may respond by suspending compliance with that provision

(E) A state that has been directly affected by the breach may respond by suspending compliance with that provision

64. Under United States law, there is no difference between a treaty and an executive agreement.

(A) TRUE

(B) FALSE

65. According to its Charter, the purposes of the United Nations include:

   (A) Creating the foundations for a world government

   (B) Reaffirming fundamental human rights

   (C) Maintaining international peace and security

   (D) Promoting the economic and social advance of all peoples

   (E) (B), (C), and (D)

66. The League of Nations is:

   (A) A precursor organization to the United Nations

   (B) The United Nations organ responsible for supervising decolonization

   (C) The central organ of the European Union

   (D) The United Nations organ in charge of humanitarian interventions

   (E) Another name for the General Assembly

67. The United Nations is authorized to intervene in the domestic affairs of states whenever a majority of the General Assembly believes intervention to be necessary to promote the goals of the United Nations Charter.

   (A) TRUE

   (B) FALSE

68. If an international agreement conflicts with the UN Charter, whichever agreement was later in time will prevail.

   (A) TRUE

   (B) FALSE

69. Which of the following is not a principle organ of the UN?

   (A) The Trusteeship Council

    (B) The Human Rights Council

    (C) The International Court of Justice

    (D) The Economic and Social Council

    (E) The General Assembly

70. All of the following are part of the European Union's governing structure, except:

    (A) The Trusteeship Council

    (B) The European Parliament

    (C) The European Commission

    (D) The Court of Justice

    (E) The Council of Ministers

71. The United Nations body with primary authority for maintaining peace and security is:

    (A) The General Assembly

    (B) The International Court of Justice

    (C) The Security Council

    (D) The Secretary General's Office of Peacekeeping

    (E) The Trusteeship Council

72. Under Article VII, the Security Council may enact binding resolutions whenever it determines there is:

    (A) A threat to peace

    (B) A breach of the peace

    (C) An act of aggression

    (D) All of the above

    (E) (A) and (B) only

73. The Security Council has the power authorize the use of force in response to a breach of the peace.

    (A) TRUE

    (B) FALSE

74. The Security Council can impose economic sanctions in response to a breach of the peace.

    (A) TRUE

    (B) FALSE

75. The membership of the Security Council is composed of:

    (A) Five permanent members and ten elected members

    (B) Fifteen permanent members

    (C) Ten permanent members and five elected members

    (D) Fifteen members elected by the General Assembly

    (E) The full membership of the United Nations

76. Which of the following is a permanent member of the Security Council?

    (A) Brazil

    (B) India

    (C) France

    (D) Germany

    (E) Japan

77. To be adopted in the Security Council, a resolution (other than a procedural matter) must receive support from:

    (A) A majority of the Permanent Members and a Majority of the Elected Members (for a total of 9 votes)

    (B) Unanimous support from all 15 Security Council Members

    (C) All of the Permanent Members and a Majority of the Elected Members (for a total of 11 votes)

    (D) All of the Permanent Members and at least 4 of the Elected Members (for a total of 9 votes)

    (E) A majority of the Permanent Members and all of the Elected Members (for a total of 13 votes)

78. Critiques of the Security Council include:

    (A) Its lack of democratic accountability

(B) The ability of permanent members to veto resolutions that otherwise would be approved by a majority of members

(C) The lack of civility and level of hostility in its discussions

(D) The disproportionate power that it gives western states within the UN system

(E) (A), (B), and (D)

79. What is the Responsibility to Protect?

ANSWER:

80. The Responsibility to Protect (R2P) is a new *jus cogens* norm.

(A) TRUE

(B) FALSE

81. The UN Secretary General is:

(A) The chief administrator of the United Nations

(B) The commander in chief of the United Nations Army

(C) The chairperson of the Security Council

(D) The chairperson of the General Assembly

(E) All of the above

82. The only UN organ in which all member states have the right to be represented and vote is:

(A) The Security Council

(B) The International Court of Justice

(C) The Economic and Social Council

(D) The General Assembly

(E) The Secretariat

83. The General Assembly has authority to adopt binding international law.

(A) TRUE

(B) FALSE

84. The United Nations Charter can be amended by a majority vote in the General Assembly.

    (A) TRUE

    (B) FALSE

85. The International Labor Organization is:

    (A) A UN agency that assists domestic labor organizations by supervising union elections

    (B) A UN agency that assists employers resolve labor shortages by coordinating visas and removing barriers to economic migration

    (C) A UN agency that brings together government representatives and labor organizations in order to negotiate laws that protect workers from unfair labor practices

    (D) A UN agency that brings together labor organizations and employers for workshops and retreats intended to promote workplace harmony and discourage union busting

    (E) A UN agency that brings together representatives of governments, labor unions and employers to develop international labor standards

86. Because the power to make war is an inherent aspect of sovereignty, "just war theory" can be invoked to justify the unprovoked and aggressive use of force by one state against another.

    (A) TRUE

    (B) FALSE

87. If the United States invaded Mexico in order to annex Cancun as a part of United States territory, its actions would be:

    (A) Illegal under international law unless the United States invoked the right of conquest to justify its actions

    (B) Illegal under international law regardless of any justifications offered by the United States

    (C) Illegal under international law unless the United States invoked the right of self-defense to justify its actions

    (D) Illegal under international law unless the United States could prove that this action was necessary to stop the flow of illegal drugs across the US-Mexican border

    (E) Both (C) and (D)

88. Under the UN Charter, the use of force is always illegal.

    (A) TRUE

    (B) FALSE

89. The term *jus ad bellum* refers to:

    (A) The law that is applicable during wartime

    (B) The law governing the right to use force

    (C) The law governing peace treaties that end an armed conflict

    (D) All of the above

    (E) None of the above

90. Even if a state is not a member of the United Nations, it is still bound by *jus ad bellum* and therefore is not free to use force as it sees fit.

    (A) TRUE

    (B) FALSE

91. The use of force in self-defense is wholly an individual prerogative of states.

    (A) TRUE

    (B) FALSE

92. Among the international law justifications for the Iraq War offered by the United States were:

    (A) The inherent right of anticipatory Self-Defense

    (B) Prior authorization by the Security Council

    (C) The inherent right of conquest

    (D) All of the above

    (E) (A) and (B) only

93. The Convention to Ban Landmines holds a unique place among multilateral treaties because:

    (A) It was ratified extremely quickly and the treaty originated in civil society

    (B) It limits the power of the Security Council to authorize aggressive force

    (C) It is the only treaty aside from the UN Charter that has universal participation

    (D) It is the only treaty that bans a specific weapon of war

    (E) All of the above

94. The term international humanitarian law includes:

    (A) The permissibility of the use of force

    (B) The conduct of hostilities

    (C) The terms of peace treaties to end hostilities

    (D) (A) and (B) only

    (E) (A), (B) and (C)

95. If a state resorts to the use of force in circumstances deemed unlawful under the UN Charter, international humanitarian law does not apply to the conflict

    (A) TRUE

    (B) FALSE

96. The rights and obligations under international humanitarian law are:

    (A) Reciprocal. Therefore, if an international humanitarian law obligation is violated by one party to a conflict, all other parties to the conflict are no longer bound by international humanitarian law.

    (B) Reciprocal. Therefore, if an international humanitarian law obligation is violated by one party to a conflict, other parties to the conflict are no longer bound by international humanitarian law with regard to the breaching party.

    (C) Independent. Therefore, each party to a conflict is bound by the obligations of international humanitarian law regardless of the conduct of other parties.

    (D) Semi-reciprocal. Therefore, if an international humanitarian law obligation is violated by one party to a conflict, all other parties to the conflict are no longer bound by that particular humanitarian law obligation, but all other obligations remain intact.

    (E) Semi-reciprocal. Therefore, if an international humanitarian law obligation is violated by one party to a conflict, other parties to the conflict are no longer bound by that particular international humanitarian law with regard to the breaching party. The obligation remains intact with regard to all other parties to the conflict, and all other international humanitarian law obligations remain intact.

97. International humanitarian law applies to any international conflict, whether or not there is a declaration of war.

    (A) TRUE

    (B) FALSE

98. The Geneva Conventions lay out the international humanitarian law obligations toward:

    (A) Wounded and sick members of armed forces in the field

    (B) Wounded and sick members of armed forces at sea

    (C) Prisoners of war

    (D) Civilians during time of war

    (E) All of the above

99. International humanitarian law applies only to international conflicts. Its obligations therefore are not triggered by a wholly intrastate conflict.

    (A) TRUE

    (B) FALSE

100. Conflicts with non-state actors, like terrorist groups, are not covered by humanitarian law.

    (A) TRUE

    (B) FALSE

101. Among the actions prohibited by Common Article 3 of the Geneva Conventions are:

    (A) Cruel treatment and torture

    (B) Taking of hostages

    (C) Outrages to personal dignity, which include humiliating and degrading treatment

    (D) Sentencing or executing prisoners without first conducting judicial proceedings in a regularly constituted court

    (E) All of the above

102. Despite the lack of any enforcement language in Common Article 3, international tribunals have asserted jurisdiction over Article 3 violations.

    (A) TRUE

    (B) FALSE

103. Among the key principles of international humanitarian law are:

   (A) Belligerents do not have unlimited choice of means to attack

   (B) The distinction between combatants and noncombatants must be respected

   (C) Noncombatants (whether civilian, POW or wounded) must be treated with humanity

   (D) Attacks must be directed at military targets

   (E) All of the above

104. The terms Hague Law and Geneva Law are synonymous — both referring to hostilities that can be conducted in a lawful manner.

   (A) TRUE

   (B) FALSE

105. International Humanitarian law bans the use of certain types of weapons, including:

   (A) Poison and asphyxiating gasses

   (B) Expanding bullets

   (C) Biological weapons

   (D) Chemical weapons

   (E) All of the above

106. International humanitarian law:

   (A) Bans all use of nuclear weapons

   (B) Bans all use and stockpiling of nuclear weapons

   (C) Applies to the use of nuclear weapons but may not ban the use of such weapons in extreme situations

   (D) Applies to the use of nuclear weapons and allows their use

   (E) Does not apply to the use of nuclear weapons at all

107. The use of disproportionate force can constitute a war crime under international law. In this context, the principle of proportionality means:

   (A) Belligerents must not launch an attack likely to result in civilian deaths that are clearly excessive in relation to the anticipated military advantage

   (B) Belligerents must not launch an attack likely to result in the death of civilians

(C) Belligerents must not launch an attack directed against civilians

(D) Belligerents must not use air strikes against artillery positions

(E) All of the above

108. Grave breaches of the Geneva Conventions include:

(A) Willful killing

(B) Torture or inhuman treatment

(C) Willfully causing serious injury to body or health

(D) Extensive destruction or appropriation of property

(E) All of the above

109. The Geneva Conventions contain no enforcement mechanism.

(A) TRUE

(B) FALSE

110. Universal jurisdiction may be used by any State to prosecute the current head of another state, when that individual is alleged to have committed grave breaches of the Geneva Conventions.

(A) TRUE

(B) FALSE

111. The International Red Cross has official status and delegated responsibilities under the Geneva Conventions.

(A) TRUE

(B) FALSE

112. The Martens clause specifies that:

(A) Only positive law, in the form of treaties, can create international humanitarian law obligations

(B) Decisions of the UN Security Council can create international humanitarian law obligations

(C) Domestic law, when more protective than international law, can create international humanitarian law obligations

(D) In the absence of specific treaty provisions, general international law continues to govern international humanitarian law obligations

(E)   None of the above

113.   The Geneva Conventions contain the international rules:

   (A)   Limiting the conduct of states with regard to prisoners of war

   (B)   Limiting the conduct of states with regard to permissible weapons of war

   (C)   Limiting the conduct of states with regard to noncombatants

   (D)   Limiting the conduct of states with regard to methods of warfare

   (E)   All of the above

114.   Humanitarian Intervention:

   (A)   Is a long-standing principle of international law that dates back to the League of Nations

   (B)   Is strictly prohibited under international law

   (C)   Was NATO's explanation for its use of force in the Former Yugoslavia

   (D)   Was a principle justification for European colonialist expansion

   (E)   Has only been tried with prior Security Council Authorization

115. The International Criminal Court's jurisdiction includes:

    (A) Crimes with an international dimension like drug trafficking, smuggling and fraud

    (B) Prosecution of human rights abuses that occur anywhere in the world

    (C) Appeals from national courts whenever those courts apply international criminal law

    (D) Genocide and other systematic crimes when carried out as official policy during war

    (E) All of the above

116. Among the crimes within the purview of the International Criminal Court are:

    (A) Genocide

    (B) Crimes against humanity

    (C) War crimes

    (D) Aggression

    (E) All of the above

117. Genocide means:

ANSWER:

118. The crime of aggression is well-defined under international law.

    (A) TRUE

    (B) FALSE

119. The term "crimes against humanity" means:

ANSWER:

120. The term "war crimes" means:

ANSWER:

121. An International Criminal Court investigation and prosecution will displace and take precedence over a comparable state proceeding whenever a crime within the court's jurisdiction is alleged to have occurred.

    (A) TRUE

    (B) FALSE

122. Complementarity means that:

ANSWER:

123. The International Criminal Court is an organ of the United Nations.

    (A) TRUE

    (B) FALSE

124. The International Criminal Court has jurisdiction over:

    (A) States as criminal defendants

    (B) Corporations and other legal persons as criminal defendants

    (C) Natural persons as criminal defendants

    (D) (B) and (C) only

    (E) (A), (B), and (C)

125. Under the Rome Statute, a person can be criminally responsible and liable for punishment for a crime within the jurisdiction of the Court if that person:

    (A) Committed a crime listed in Article 5, whether as an individual or jointly with another person

    (B) Ordered, solicited or induced the commission of a crime listed in Article 5, when the crime in fact occurs or is attempted

    (C) Aided, abetted or otherwise assisted in the commission of a crime listed in Article 5 or its attempted commission

    (D) Attempted to commit a crime listed in Article 5 by taking a substantial step toward its execution, even if the crime did not occur because of circumstances independent of the person's intentions

    (E) All of the actions listed above could bring a person within the jurisdiction of the ICC

126. Incitement to genocide is a crime under the jurisdiction of the ICC.

   (A) TRUE

   (B) FALSE

127. International human rights:

(A) Can only be enforced by the United Nations

(B) Can only be enforced by States

(C) Can be enforced by States and by the United Nations but do not apply to citizens of states that object

(D) Can be enforced by states and by the United Nations, and apply to all human beings regardless of their citizenship

(E) Are not enforceable

128. What is the purpose of International Human Rights Law?

(A) To protect citizens from actions of their government

(B) To protect individuals from the actions of non-state actors

(C) To protect individuals and sometimes groups from actions taken by governments

(D) To protect individuals from actions taken by other individuals

(E) To provide fodder for discussion at the UN General Assembly

129. Individuals have human rights when they are outside of their own countries.

(A) TRUE

(B) FALSE

130. When did international human rights emerge as an international legal doctrine?

(A) In the earliest records of human history

(B) In 1948 with the adoption of the Universal Declaration of Human Rights

(C) In 1966 with the adoption of the Covenant on Civil and Political Rights

(D) In 1989 after the fall of the Berlin Wall

(E) In 2005 as a result of the World Summit

131. The UN Charter guarantees human rights to individuals.

    (A) TRUE

    (B) FALSE

132. Questions of expropriation under international law are governed by:

    (A) International law

    (B) State domestic law

    (C) Both state domestic law and international law, but in case of conflict state law trumps

    (D) The arbitration rules adopted by the New York Convention of 1958

    (E) There are no rules governing questions of expropriation under international law

133. How does the law of State Responsibility for Injuries to Aliens differ from International Human Rights law?

    (A) The two doctrines have converged and are now identical

    (B) International Human Rights Law protects individuals only when their nationality is that of the offending state, while the law of State Responsibility for Injuries to Aliens applies only to non-nationals

    (C) The law of State Responsibility protects individuals as well as corporations and other legal persons while Human Rights law only protects natural persons

    (D) International Human Rights Law protects individuals only when their nationality is not that of the offending state while the law of State Responsibility for Injuries to Aliens applies only to nationals

    (E) The law of State Responsibility protects only natural persons, while Human Rights law protects individuals as well as corporations and other legal persons

134. Under the doctrine of State Responsibility for Injuries to Aliens, where does a cause of action lie when a foreign government subjects an individual to treatment that violates international law?

    (A) With the individual

    (B) With the state of nationality

    (C) With the UN Security Council

    (D) With the UN High Commissioner for Human Rights

    (E) With all of the above

135. What substantive law applies to state claims on behalf of their nationals injured by the conduct of another state?

    (A) Multilateral and bilateral treaties to which the states are parties

    (B) The general principles of law recognized by civilized nations

    (C) Both (A) and (B)

    (D) Neither (A) nor (B)

    (E) Only the Draft Articles on the Responsibility of States for Internationally Wrongful Acts

136. Before a state can be held responsible for any action, it is necessary to prove:

    (A) That the act is attributable to the state under international law

    (B) That the act constituted the breach of an international obligation on the part of the state.

    (C) That the act occurred less than 3 years before the claim asserted was filed

    (D) Both (A) and (B)

    (E) (A), (B), and (C)

137. The Universal Declaration of Human Rights is arguably binding because:

    (A) It is a binding treaty that was ratified by the General Assembly

    (B) It is an authoritative interpretation of the UN Charter provisions on human rights

    (C) It has become customary international law

    (D) Both (B) and (C)

    (E) All of the above.

138. The Universal Declaration states that its provisions apply to:

    (A) Citizens of states that have ratified the Declaration only

    (B) Adults only

    (C) Everyone

    (D) Men only

    (E) Discrete and insular minorities only

139. Among its provisions, the Universal Declaration provides that "everyone" has the right to:

    (A) Life, liberty and security of person

(B) Recognition as a person before the law

(C) An effective remedy by competent tribunals for violations of fundamental rights

(D) All of the above

(E) None of the above

140. The Universal Declaration does not provide that "everyone" has the right to:

(A) Freedom of movement in order to pursue one's livelihood

(B) Freedom of movement within a state

(C) Freedom of movement to leave any country and return to one's own country

(D) All of the above

(E) None of the above

141. All of the rights articulated in the Universal Declaration have been fully realized in international law.

(A) TRUE

(B) FALSE

142. State parties are required to implement the rights contained in the International Covenant on Civil and Political Rights:

(A) Immediately upon ratification

(B) Progressively over time

(C) With all deliberate speed

(D) Within 10 years of ratification

(E) Never because states have no binding commitments under the Covenant

143. A major critique of international human rights, as currently implemented, is that it places too much emphasis on social and economic rights at the expense of political and civil rights.

(A) TRUE

(B) FALSE

144. State parties are required to implement the rights contained in the International Covenant on Economic, Social and Cultural rights:

(A) Immediately upon ratification

(B) Progressively over time

(C) With all deliberate speed

(D) Within 10 years of ratification

(E) Never because states have no binding commitments under the Covenant

145. Negative rights include those basic rights that a state is obligated to provide to all inhabitants in order to maintain a minimum quality of life.

(A) TRUE

(B) FALSE

146. One of the major criticisms of the intellectual underpinnings of international human rights law is that:

(A) It places too much emphasis on community

(B) It emphasizes cultural relativism rather than universality

(C) It elevates individual rights over all other kinds of rights

(D) It focuses on social and economic rights to the exclusion of political and civil rights

(E) All of the above

147. The UN Economic and Social Council is empowered to enforce the ICESCR through adjudication and sanctions.

(A) TRUE

(B) FALSE

148. There is no way for individuals or states to make complaints under the ICCPR or the ICESCR.

(A) TRUE

(B) FALSE

149. Perhaps the most significant limitation on the effectiveness of international human rights agreements is:

(A) The internal political agendas of states, which may or may not coincide with international human rights principles

(B) The competition between groups that might benefit from implementation of international human rights agreements

(C) The lack of a forum and organization for discussing international human rights

(D) The machinations of powerful NGOs to suppress the discussion of international human rights

(E) All of the above

150. The UN Human Rights Council was created to:

(A) Identify states to target for human rights investigations and conduct prosecutions of responsible individuals within those states

(B) Adjudicate cases of human rights violations in Rwanda and the former Yugoslavia

(C) Undertake universal periodic review of the human rights records of all states

(D) Recommend measures to the General Assembly for the further development of international human rights law

(E) Both (C) and (D)

151. Helga, a citizen of Germany, believes that her human rights have been violated because her marriage to her same-sex partner Vera is not recognized under German law. She thinks this unequal treatment of marriages between same-sex and opposite-sex couples violates the right to family guaranteed in Article 8(1) of the European Convention on Human Rights, and also violates the prohibition on government interference with the family found in Article 8(2). Having unsuccessfully pursued her claim through domestic channels, she would like to bring a claim at the European level. She may elect either to bring this claim before the European Court of Justice or the European Court of Human Rights because both have jurisdiction.

(A) TRUE

(B) FALSE

152. Regional Human Rights agreements are intended to supplant domestic court jurisdiction over allegations involving human rights violations.

(A) TRUE

(B) FALSE

153. The European Court of Human Rights is not part of the European Union.

(A) TRUE

(B) FALSE

154. Individuals cannot refer cases to the European Court of Human Rights.

(A) TRUE

(B) FALSE

155. The European Court of Human Rights has jurisdiction over:

    (A) Actions of European States and companies everywhere in the world alleged to violate rights enumerated in the European Convention

    (B) Actions of European States and companies within Europe alleged to violate rights enumerated in the European Convention

    (C) Actions alleged to violate rights enumerated in the European Convention, regardless of where they occur or who commits them

    (D) Actions alleged to violate rights enumerated in the European Convention, regardless of who commits them, so long as the actions occur within the territory of a High Contracting Party

    (E) Actions alleged to violate rights enumerated in the European Convention, committed by a High Contracting Party that occurs within the territory of a High Contracting Party

156. The Charter of Fundamental Freedoms and the European Convention and the European Convention on Human Rights guarantee a slightly different set of rights, and residents of the European Union can have recourse to both.

    (A) TRUE

    (B) FALSE

157. A state can be a member of the Organization of American States without accepting the jurisdiction of the Inter-American Court of Human Rights.

    (A) TRUE

    (B) FALSE

158. The Inter-American Commission on Human Rights has jurisdiction:

    (A) Over all individual petitions directed at state parties, but not over inter-state petitions

    (B) Over all inter-state petitions directed at state parties, but not over individual petitions

    (C) Over all inter-state petitions but has jurisdiction over individual petitions only if a state has consented to such jurisdiction

    (D) Over all individual petitions but has jurisdiction over inter-state petitions only if a state has consented to such jurisdiction

    (E) Over all individual and all inter-state petitions

159. The African Charter recognizes and protects both individual and group rights.

    (A) TRUE

(B) FALSE

160. The Millennium Development Goals set a target of reaching 8 identified anti-poverty goals by 2015, including:

(A) Halving the number of people who live on less than $1 per day

(B) Ensuring that all children are able to complete a course of primary education

(C) Reducing under-five childhood mortality by 2/3

(D) Halting and reversing the spread of malaria and HIV

(E) All of the above

161. The Millennium Development Goals are identical with human rights.

(A) TRUE

(B) FALSE

162. The 2007 Declaration on the Rights of Indigenous Peoples is the first international agreement dealing with indigenous peoples.

(A) TRUE

(B) FALSE

163. How does international law distinguish between a colonized people and an indigenous people?

ANSWER:

164. International Labor Organization (ILO) Convention 107 does not guarantee indigenous people the right to retain their own customs and institutions distinct from the laws of the state in which they are situated.

(A) TRUE

(B) FALSE

165. The Declaration on the Rights of Indigenous Peoples:

(A) Is a duly ratified treaty and is therefore binding on all members of the United Nations

(B) Is a restatement of customary law and is therefore binding on all members of the United Nations

(C) Is a duly ratified treaty and is therefore binding on parties that have ratified the treaty

(D) Is non-binding soft law, but bolsters state obligations to indigenous peoples under customary international law

(E) Is a general principle of international law

166. The Declaration on the Rights of Indigenous Peoples vests indigenous populations with the absolute right to self-determination.

(A) TRUE

(B) FALSE

167. The Convention on Biodiversity guaranteed control over natural resources to indigenous peoples who are dependent on those resources and who were historically responsible for their exploitation and conservation.

    (A) TRUE

    (B) FALSE

168. Environmental Law became a significant part of international law:

    (A) In the 19th Century as states began to grapple with the side effects of their newly industrialized economies

    (B) During World War I, as part of the League of Nations

    (C) After World War II, with the birth of the United Nations

    (D) After the 1972 Stockholm Declaration on the Human Environment

    (E) After the success of the Copenhagen Accord on Greenhouse Gas Emissions

169. If Canada wanted to build an extremely polluting industrial facility on its border with the United States, commonly accepted principles of sovereignty mean that the United States would have no recourse under international law for any pollution that it suffered as a result of Canada constructing and operating that facility.

    (A) TRUE

    (B) FALSE

170. Intergenerational equity, the idea of fairness to future generations in environmental decision making:

    (A) Has become a *jus cogens* norm

    (B) Is a critical principle in many multilateral environmental agreements

    (C) Is well-accepted as a basic human right

    (D) All of the above

    (E) None of the above

171. The "race to the bottom" refers to:

    (A) The tendency of states in a global trade regime to degrade their environmental standards in order to gain a competitive advantage in the world economic arena

    (B) The tendency of states in a global trade regime to introduce more stringent environmental laws

(C) The tendency of states in a global trade regime to direct more funds toward enforcing domestic environmental laws

(D) The tendency of states in a global trade regime to cooperate in order to improve their domestic environmental laws

(E) The tendency of states in a global trade regime to incorporate environmental protection into trade rules

172. Sustainable development is defined in international law as:

(A) Development that recognizes the links between world peace and increased global economic prosperity

(B) Development that promotes tourism in order to promote economic prosperity

(C) Development that meets the needs of the present generation without compromising the ability of future generations to meet their own needs

(D) Development that gives non-governmental organizations a prominent decision making role

(E) None of the above

173. Sammy Snakeskin wants to import extremely rare rhinoceros horns to China to supply a thriving market for traditional medicine. Rhinoceros are an endangered species, listed in Appendix I of the Convention on International Trade in Endangered Species (CITES) which prohibits international trade in listed species. But Sammy does not believe that international law is really law, and he is attracted by the profit he can make from selling the horns. He hires some hunters to track and kill rhinos in Zimbabwe. They deliver the horns to Sammy who places the horns in his luggage and tries to board a plane to China. He is arrested by customs officials who claim to be enforcing international law. His arrest was probably based on:

(A) Domestic law adopted to implement state obligations under CITES

(B) Interpol's enforcement powers, which under CITES allows them to make arrests for violations of Annex I

(C) The precedent set by the Trail Smelter Arbitration

(D) The NGO TRAFFIC's specially designated enforcement authority under CITES

(E) Direct international enforcement of CITES by UN police officers stationed at "high risk borders"

174. The Rio Declaration is binding international law.

(A) TRUE

(B) FALSE

175. The Precautionary Principle:

   (A)   Demands that states refrain from an action unless they are sure that the action will not cause any harm to the environment

   (B)   Requires that before states engage in activities likely to create cross-border harms they first reach an agreement with other states about paying compensation for those harms

   (C)   Counsels that lack of scientific certainty is not a reason to postpone cost effective measures to prevent or minimize environmental harm

   (D)   Prevents states from engaging in risky activities unless they can demonstrate that they have taken all available steps to minimize or avoid environmental harm

   (E)   All of the above

176. *Common but differentiated responsibility* means that states responsible for the past economic exploitation of global commons have an enhanced responsibility to remedy or mitigate the consequences of that exploitation.

   (A)   TRUE

   (B)   FALSE

177. There is never a problem with overlapping jurisdictions in international environmental law.

   (A)   TRUE

   (B)   FALSE

178. A Framework Convention is a multi-lateral treaty that:

   (A)   Specifies all of the details of the agreement between the parties thus ensuring that no further agreements will be necessary on the topic

   (B)   Specifies the principles by which later annexes, protocols, or schedules will flesh out details of implementation, specify standards, and otherwise elaborate on the initial framework agreement

   (C)   Has no binding force and merely commits the parties to negotiate in good faith

   (D)   Takes the law of one jurisdiction as a model to be followed by the rest of the world

   (E)   None of the above

179. Institutions that have helped shape the contours of international environmental law and regulation include:

   (A)   The General Assembly

   (B)   The Global Environmental Facility

(C) The UN Environmental Programme

(D) All of the above

(E) None of the above

180. Suppose that the nation of New Marco wishes to build a lead smelter on the river that forms its border with the nation of Old Amster. Old Amster believes that New Marco has not conducted an adequate environmental impact assessment (EIA) and that the smelter will seriously harm Old Amster's environment. Almost 70 years ago, the two states negotiated a treaty governing shared uses of the river, but the treaty is silent about environmental issues. Does Old Amster have any claim under international law?

(A) Yes. The Espoo Convention specifies that states must conduct EIAs whenever their activities might have transboundary environmental impacts.

(B) No. EIAs are wholly a matter of domestic law. So long as New Marco complied with its domestic law, Old Amster has no ground for complaint.

(C) Yes. The Rio Declaration requires that states conduct EIAs.

(D) No. International law governing EIAs applies only to general plans and not to specific projects.

(E) Yes, to the extent that EIAs have become a part of customary international law.

181. Green accounting is a way to calculate a more comprehensive picture of a country's overall wealth by placing traditional GDP calculations in the context of a country's degradation or accumulation of human and natural capital.

(A) TRUE

(B) FALSE

182. There is little or no overlap between international environmental law and international human rights law.

(A) TRUE

(B) FALSE

183. The Intergovernmental Panel on Climate Change (IPCC) is an organization that:

(A) Issues scientific Assessments and Reports offering observations and conclusions about greenhouse gas concentrations in the atmosphere

(B) Drafts proposed domestic law intended to combat climate change and lobbies national governments to adopt those laws

(C) Lobbies Congress to fund alternative energy programs

(D) All of the above

(E) None of the above

184. The IPCC has concluded that increases in average global temperature since the mid-20th century are slight or non-existent, and are likely due to natural variation in the earth's weather cycles.

(A) TRUE

(B) FALSE

185. The 2005 Millennium Assessment concluded that:

(A) The function of the world's ecosystems changed more rapidly in the second half of the 20th century than in all previous recorded history

(B) The number of species is declining rapidly and almost 30% of mammals, birds and amphibians are threatened or endangered

(C) Ecological degradation associated with urbanization and food production threatens the health of millions of people

(D) All of the above

(E) None of the above

186. Vessels on the high seas have traditionally been viewed as wholly outside the jurisdiction of any state.

    (A) TRUE

    (B) FALSE

187. In 1945, when President Truman extended United States control over all natural resources on its continental shelf, he invoked:

    (A) The customary international law principle of *mare liberum*

    (B) The customary international law principle of *mare clausum*

    (C) The customary international law principle of a state's right to protect its natural resources

    (D) All of the above

    (E) None of the above

188. Under the Law of the Sea Convention, a state may declare an Exclusive Economic Zone (EEZ):

    (A) That extends as far as the state's continental shelf

    (B) That extends up to 200 nautical miles from the coastal baseline

    (C) That extends up to 12 nautical miles from the coastal baseline

    (D) Only with the prior permission of the International Seabed Authority

    (E) That extends as far into the sea as the state can control from land

189. Jane Doe, a citizen of Costa Rica, owns a fishing vessel called the Jolly Raymond. Each year, the Jolly Raymond travels throughout the Caribbean Sea, fishing for various fish which are then sold in Costa Rican markets. Therefore, the Jolly Raymond:

    (A) Must be flagged as a Costa Rican ship because a ship must fly the flag that corresponds to its owner's nationality

    (B) Must fly the flag of a Caribbean Nation because a ship can only be flagged by a State in the region in which it operates

(C) Need not fly any State's flag because vessels do not have a nationality

(D) Can fly the flag of any State willing to flag it

(E) Will have to switch its flag each time it enters the waters of a different state

190. The Destiny, an Algerian flagged vessel, and the Fate, a Dutch flagged vessel are involved in a collision on the high seas. There are serious injuries to crew on both vessels, and significant property damage. In addition, the collision created an oil spill and possibly dumped other pollutants into the ocean. The collision is probably the result of criminal activity on the part of one or both of the vessels. Who may exercise criminal jurisdiction over the incident?

(A) The flag State of each vessel may exercise criminal jurisdiction over its own vessel, but has no authority over the other vessel involved in the incident

(B) The flag State of either vessel may exercise criminal jurisdiction and may board both vessels in order to investigate

(C) There is no possibility of criminal jurisdiction because the incident occurred on the high seas

(D) The nearest coastal State can exercise criminal jurisdiction over both ships

(E) Only the United Nations will have criminal jurisdiction because the incident occurred on the high seas

191. Even though Canada has sovereignty over its territorial seas, it must nonetheless allow the ships of all states the right of "innocent passage."

(A) TRUE

(B) FALSE

192. A State has total sovereignty over its continental shelf and exclusive economic zone.

(A) TRUE

(B) FALSE

193. Australia's fishing industry is in deep trouble because years of overfishing have depleted available fish populations. In order to prevent a total collapse of its fisheries, Australia would like to create "no-take" zones and limit access to the fishery to properly licensed boats that will each be assigned a strict quota. Fishing beyond the quota may result in forfeiture of the boat. Other fishing nations, including Tonga object to this regime. Tonga is particularly upset because its boats are not being issued quotas, and the "no take" zones are in areas that Tongan boats often fished in the past. Under UNCLOS, which of the following best state's Australia's authority to implement its fishing plan?

(A) Australia may control fishing activities only in an area of up to 24 nautical miles from its coastal baseline

(B) Australia may control fishing activities only in an area of up to 200 nautical miles from its coastal baseline

(C) Australia may control fishing activities only in an area of up to 12 nautical miles from its coastal baseline

(D) Australia may control fishing activities only in an area that extends as far as its continental shelf

(E) Australia may control fishing activities only in its internal waters

194. Under UNCLOS, Haiti has claims to a continental shelf of about 5000 sq. km. However, Haiti is a desperately poor country with little capacity to exploit resources found on its continental shelf. If Haiti does not exercise its sovereign rights to explore and develop the mineral resources of its continental shelf, another State can step in and do so.

(A) TRUE

(B) FALSE

195. If there are overlaps or conflicts between the claims to territorial seas or EEZs that two or more states would otherwise be entitled to make under UNCLOS:

(A) The first State to declare these territories gets preference, creating a problem of a race to file

(B) Neither State has jurisdiction over the area of overlap, which is instead considered to be part of the "common heritage of humanity"

(C) The States involved can either negotiate a delimitation agreement or might elect to refer the issue to the ICJ

(D) The State with the larger EEZ is expected to yield its claim in favor of the State with the smaller EEZ

(E) The States are expected to split the territory equally, regardless of the configuration of their respective coastlines.

196. The "Area" refers to:

(A) The seabed and ocean floor beyond the limits of national jurisdiction

(B) The continental shelf around Antarctica over which no sovereign claims may be made

(C) The traditional 3 mile territorial sea, now subsumed within the 12 mile territorial sea recognized by UNCLOS

(D) The region between Bermuda, Florida and Puerto Rico where a number of aircraft and surface vessels have disappeared under mysterious circumstances

(E) The newly-open shipping route in the Arctic that has emerged as a result of climate change

197. Climate change is having a large impact on the Arctic. Among the more visible of these impacts is the retreat of sea ice. As a result of these changing conditions, shipping through the fabled Northwest Passage may become a reality over the next few years. Canada is deeply alarmed by this prospect. Which of the following arguments might Canada make in a bid to prevent shipping:

(A) The newly-exposed waters are internal Canadian waters

(B) The newly-exposed waters are archipelagic waters

(C) The newly-exposed waters are an international strait

(D) All of the above

(E) (A) and (B) only

198. The Law of the Sea Convention is generally recognized as customary international law.

(A) TRUE

(B) FALSE

199. If Uganda, a landlocked state, wants to develop a maritime fishing industry:

(A) It can use the principles of the sovereign equality of states to demand an EEZ of its own, even though it is landlocked

(B) Ugandan vessels can only fish on the high seas and can never fish in any state's EEZ

(C) Ugandan vessels can fish on the high seas or within the EEZ of states that allow it access

(D) It will be unable to do so, because as a landlocked country it has no rights to fish in the oceans

(E) None of the above

200. Submarines must always surface and display their flags when transiting the territorial sea of another State but not when transiting international straits.

(A) TRUE

(B) FALSE

201. The International Tribunal for the Law of the Sea has exclusive jurisdiction to resolve disputes that arise under the Law of the Sea Treaty.

(A) TRUE

(B) FALSE

202. With regard to fish stocks that straddle the EEZs of two or more states, or the EEZ of a state and the high seas:

(A) Each coastal state is free to do as it pleases because the state has sovereign rights over living marine resources within the EEZ

(B) States commit to coordinate by following the lead of the coastal state with the largest percentage of the fish stock within its EEZ (the dominant state)

(C) States commit to coordinate by forming and complying with regional fisheries agreements and regional fisheries organizations

(D) States commit to complying with regional fisheries agreements where they exist, or to follow the lead of the dominant state if there is no relevant agreement

(E) None of the above

203. When the World Trade Organization (WTO) came into existence, the General Agreement on Tariffs and Trade (GATT) ceased to be binding international law.

(A) TRUE

(B) FALSE

204. The most innovative feature of the WTO is:

(A) The dispute settlement process which makes dispute resolution decisions enforceable

(B) The WTO police force which enables the WTO to unilaterally enforce the trade agreements

(C) The public outreach and education process which ensures that WTO principles of free trade are taught in schools around the world

(D) The benefit sharing process which ensures that the benefits of trade are shared equitably across member states

(E) The negotiating process which streamlines international negotiation to allow for rapid treaty modification

205. Which of the following agreements does the WTO administer:

(A) Only the General Agreement on Tariffs and Trade (GATT)

(B) Only the GATT, and the General Agreement on Trade in Services (GATS)

(C) The GATT, the GATS, and the Agreement on Trade Related Aspects of Intellectual Property (TRIPS)

(D) The GATT, the GATS, TRIPS and the Multilateral Agreement on Investment (MIA)

(E) None of the above

206. The key difference between the WTO version of the GATT and its earlier incarnation is that:

(A) States can now block adoption of a dispute resolution ruling

(B) States can no longer block adoption of a dispute resolution ruling

(C)   States are now encouraged to negotiate bilateral trade agreements

(D)   States are now required to negotiate bilateral trade agreements

(E)   States are now forbidden to negotiate bilateral trade agreements

207. The WTO's Dispute Settlement Body (DSB) sits in panels of three to accept briefing, hear arguments and resolve each case before it.

(A)   TRUE

(B)   FALSE

208. Which of the following can initiate a dispute resolution proceeding under WTO rules:

(A)   All Member States

(B)   All States

(C)   All States and Intergovernmental Organizations

(D)   All States, Intergovernmental Organizations, and Aggrieved Natural Persons

(E)   All States, Intergovernmental Organizations, Aggrieved Natural and Juridical Persons

209. WTO dispute resolution proceedings are limited to the named parties. As a consequence, Member States that are Third Parties to a dispute before the Dispute Settlement Body are prohibited from submitting briefing or otherwise joining the WTO dispute resolution proceedings.

(A)   TRUE

(B)   FALSE

210. After a WTO panel recommendation is adopted by the Dispute Settlement Body, the parties must proceed directly to the implementation phase.

(A)   TRUE

(B)   FALSE

211. Seabird populations are increasingly threatened by overfishing. The phoenix, in particular is severely endangered, and has been listed under CITES. The United States wishes to protect all sea birds, particularly the phoenix. It passes a domestic law called the Phoenix Act. This act takes a number of measures intended to protect phoenix populations. Because of high phoenix mortality associated with drift-net fishing, Article 4 of the Act bans drift-nets within the United States EEZ. Article 5 of the Act also bans the import of fish caught by drift-net fishing. Mexico and Thailand, both major drift-net fishing states, challenge this law as an unfair trade practice under the WTO. They claim that the United States law imposes a non-tariff trade barrier in contravention of GATT requirements. Which best states the state of WTO law vis-à-vis this kind of environmental protection

measure?

(A) Article XI of the GATT provides extensive scope for domestic environmental regulations that are alleged to infringe on free trade

(B) Article XX of the GATT provides extensive scope for domestic environmental regulations that are alleged to infringe on free trade

(C) Article XI of the GATT provides a limited scope for domestic environmental regulations that are alleged to infringe on free trade

(D) Article XX of the GATT provides a limited scope for domestic environmental regulations that are alleged to infringe on free trade

(E) The GATT always overrules domestic environmental regulations alleged to infringe on free trade

PRACTICE FINAL EXAM: ESSAY QUESTION

212. For centuries, humans hunted Jabberwockies for food. With the dawn of the industrial era, Jabberwockies became a key source of oil and other raw materials. Jabberwocky hunting became an industry rather than a subsistence practice. Technological advances in the 19th century and early 20th century meant that Jabberwockies could be killed and processed in unprecedented numbers. The relentless demand for more raw materials drove many Jabberwocky species to the brink of extinction. Multiple Jabberwocky hunting nations took catches far exceeding any sustainable harvest limits. By the 1930s, more than 150,000 Jabberwockies were being killed each year, and Jabberwocky populations were dwindling. In 1945 almost 1,000,000 Jabberwockies were killed. In response to these developments, in 1946, sixteen States signed and ratified the International Convention for the Regulation of Jabberwocky Hunting (ICRJH). The ICRJH's most significant provision is Article 11, which imposes a moratorium on Jabberwocky hunting for 100 years. Since the implementation of the moratorium under the ICRJH, Jabberwocky catches have plummeted to below 1,000 per year. Nevertheless, seven of thirteen Jabberwocky species remain endangered, with two listed under CITES Appendix 1.

Among the original signatories to the ICRJH were Canada, New Zealand, and the United States. Canada's commitment to the ICRJH was accompanied by one reservation. Another 74 States have since signed the ICRJH, including Japan and Argentina. Japan signed and ratified the convention in 1986. Argentina also signed the convention in 1986 but still has not ratified it. Iceland never signed the convention. Iceland has a commercial Jabberwocky industry that sells Jabberwocky meat domestically and in Japan.

New Zealand has extensive domestic laws making it a crime to hunt, kill, harass or otherwise harm Jabberwockies. Possession of a Jabberwocky carcass is also a criminal violation. In 1994, the ICRJH voted to declare most of the high seas around Antarctica the Southern Ocean Jabberwocky Sanctuary. Japan and Iceland were the only votes against the Jabberwocky sanctuary. Neither state filed a formal objection to the designation. Recently Japanese boats have been flouting the ban on Jabberwocky hunting in the Sanctuary.

New Zealand has decided to hold violators of the ICRJH's Jabberwocky hunting moratorium responsible for what it believes to be international wrongful acts. It has demanded that the alleged violators cease their wrongful Jabberwocky hunting and it has threatened to take various unilateral countermeasures against these states:

1. **Canada for catching 10 Jabberwockies in 2010**

2. **Japan for catching 11,116 Jabberwockies in 2010**

3. **Argentina for catching 324 Jabberwockies in 2010**

4. **Iceland for catching 1,512 Jabberwockies in 2010**

Each of the States targeted as part of New Zealand's campaign has denied that it is in violation of international law, asserting the following explanations:

1. **Canada claims its Jabberwocky catch in 2010 is permitted under its reservation to the ICRJH**

2. Japan claims its Jabberwocky catch in 2010 is permitted under ICRJH Article 14

3. Argentina claims its Jabberwocky catch in 2010 is legal because it is not bound by the ICRJH moratorium

4. Iceland claims its commercial Jabberwocky catch in 2010 is legal because it is not bound by the ICRJH moratorium

You have been asked by the New Zealand foreign office to prepare a brief memo presenting your views on the legality of the targeted States' Jabberwocky hunting activities. The countermeasures that New Zealand would like to take include: trade sanctions against offending nations, boarding ships in New Zealand and international waters to search for and confiscate dead Jabberwockies, and criminal prosecutions against ship captains. [NOTE: the specific countermeasures are just FYI. Please do not analyze the legality of each of these countermeasures in your answer. Instead analyze whether New Zealand can take countermeasures at all.] Your analysis should focus on the ICRJH but be sure to point out other relevant international agreements. In preparing your memo you should rely on the following materials and your expertise in the fundamentals of public international law.

Relevant Treaty Provisions and Materials

I. International Convention for the Regulation of Jabberwocky Hunting Signed 23 June 1946 at Christchurch, New Zealand

Preamble

The Governments whose duly authorized representatives have subscribed hereto,

Recognizing the interest of the nations of the world in safeguarding for future generations the great natural resources represented by the Jabberwocky stocks;

Considering that the history of Jabberwocky hunting has seen over-fishing of one area after another and of one species of Jabberwocky after another to such a degree that it is essential to protect all species of Jabberwockies from further over-fishing;

Recognizing that it is in the common interest to achieve the optimum level of Jabberwocky stocks as rapidly as possible without causing widespread economic and nutritional distress; and

Having decided to conclude a convention to provide for the proper conservation of Jabberwocky stocks;

Have agreed as follows:

Article 11

The catch limits for the killing for commercial purposes of Jabberwockies from all stocks established pursuant to the provisions of the London Jabberwocky Hunting Treaty (1937) shall hereafter be zero. This provision will be kept under review, based upon the best scientific advice, and by 2046 at the latest the Member States will undertake a comprehensive assessment of the effects of this decision on Jabberwocky stocks and consider modification of this provision and the establishment of other catch limits.

Article 14

Notwithstanding anything contained in this Convention any Contracting Government may grant to any of its nationals a special permit authorizing that national to kill, take and treat Jabberwockies for purposes of scientific research subject to such restrictions as to number and subject to such other conditions as the Contracting Government thinks fit, and the killing, taking, and treating of Jabberwockies in accordance with the provisions of this Article shall be exempt from the operation of this Convention. Each Contracting Government may at any time revoke any such special permit which it has granted.

Article 37

Disputes arising out of the interpretation or application of the Convention shall lie within the compulsory jurisdiction of the International Court of Justice and may accordingly be brought before the Court by an application made by any party to the dispute being a Party to the Convention.

II. Canadian Reservation to the ICRJH Accompanying Canada's Ratification of the ICRJH on 28 November 1946

"Canada reserves the right, subject to its domestic environmental and cultural laws, to issue permits to recognized indigenous and native groups for up to 10 Jabberwocky catches each year for non-scientific purposes."

- Many of the ICRJH's original Member States — and all of the States that have subsequently become members have explicitly accepted the Canadian reservation.

- New Zealand explicitly objected to the Canadian reservation on 25 November 1947.

III. Extracurricular Statements and Instruments; Subsequent Conduct

- All of the ICRJH's original 16 Member States concluded a supplementary agreement at the same time they signed the ICRJH in which they defined "scientific research" — as used in ICRJH Article 14 — to mean "a very limited number of catches, the organic by-product of which may not be taken to market for consumption." Many, but not all States that subsequently became members of the ICRJH have reaffirmed this supplementary agreement.

- When it ratified the ICRJH in 1986, Japan lodged a unilateral instrument in which it declared: "Japan recognizes that the needs of science and research cannot be determined in the abstract and in advance and must be addressed as they arise. Japan further recognizes that limits on the use of the by-products of the Jabberwockies caught for scientific research constitute an unconscionable waste. Japan further asserts its intention to maintain its extensive Jabberwocky scientific research program." Twenty States that have become members of the ICRJH since 1986 — when Japan ratified the convention — have affirmed Japan's unilateral instrument.

- Since the ICRJH's entry into force, only Japan has sought to catch more than 20 Jabberwockies in one year for scientific research. Japan, however, consistently has caught more than 800 Jabberwockies each year since its ratification of the ICRJH in 1986. There has been considerable criticism of Japan in the American and European media for this practice and the non-governmental organization GreenWorld has begun to disrupt and sabotage the work of Japan's scientific Jabberwocky hunting fleet around the world. Still, until New Zealand's recent campaign, no State had formally criticized Japan for these activities.

- The official papers of the diplomatic delegations that attended the negotiations leading to the promulgation of the ICRJH have recently been made available for research. They show that a number of the Member States involved in the negotiations were stridently opposed to the moratorium's 100-year term. Many advocated a shorter time period. Letters exchanged by the diplomatic delegations, and minutes kept by a number of the delegations, reveal that the 100-year term only achieved consensus because some States felt confident that Article 14 would be given a loose definition and because it was believed that Jabberwocky stocks would recover so quickly that a protocol to the ICRJH could be negotiated lifting the moratorium in just a decade or two. For example, the United States Assistant Under-Secretary of State for Fishery Affairs wrote to several delegations during the negotiations: "As one of the post-war powers, and one of the world's most active naval and fishing States, the United States will accept the outrageously long moratorium in proposed Article 11 only with the understanding that most regular Jabberwocky hunting will be permissible under the Article 14 exception." Nevertheless, attempts by the United States and other delegations to include a broad definition of "scientific research" in the language of Article 14 were defeated.

IV. Court Decisions and Scholarship

In its advisory opinion in the case seeking clarification of the provisions of the 2001 Fukyshima Treaty on Nuclear Energy Security (the *2008 Fukyshima Treaty Advisory Opinion*), the International Court of Justice ruled that the treaty's 50-year moratorium on the use of nuclear energy must be read flexibly to permit Member States to resort to the use of nuclear energy if necessary to preserve and protect deeply-rooted cultural traditions. The ICJ used, as an example, the necessity of a potential American reliance on nuclear energy in order to keep the Las Vegas "Strip" illuminated. In reaching this conclusion the ICJ reasoned: "a prohibition of such length, and touching on such a fundamental social issue as the energy market, cannot be read in its strictest possible terms without too invasively eroding each State's sovereign equality."

Several Japanese courts have issued decisions finding the disposal of marketable organic by-products of scientific research to be "intolerable waste" that is prohibited by Japanese law.

Some scholars, including Professor Rudy Wolfrum (who is widely viewed as the world's leading expert on international maritime and fishery laws), think that the moratorium's long 100-year term is so excessive that it can only properly be read as an effort to emphasize the Member States' intention to be more conscientious about the Jabberwocky hunting industry. This interpretation of the convention counsels a broad definition of the "scientific research" exception to Article 14.

ANSWER:

ANSWERS

1. **The correct answer is (D).** Although international law was once limited to the law that governs relations between and among states (Answer (A)), contemporary conceptions of international law are much broader, including the interactions listed in Answers B-D. Therefore, **Answer (A) is too limited to be correct, as are (B) and (C). Answer (E) is incorrect** because international law does not govern the relationship between sub-national entities (like cities or states) and the nation state.

2. **The correct answer is (E).** The term Transnational Law refers to the study of law that concerns more than one state. As such, it is generally considered to embrace international law, comparative law, conflict of laws, and supranational law.

3. **The correct answer is (B).** The Peace of Westphalia of 1648 ended the Thirty Years War, and marked the establishment of the modern state with central governmental institutions that could enforce control over its inhabitants and defend them from attacks by other states. **The other answers are incorrect.** There was no single agreement that marked the end of European colonialism, or the Indian wars in the United States. Nor was there a single treaty ending World War II, but hostilities ended with Japan's surrender in 1945. The United Nations Charter created the United Nations in 1946. The Treaty of Versailles ended World War I and established the League of Nations.

4. Sovereignty is the quality of having supreme, independent control and lawmaking authority over a territory. It finds expression in the power to rule and make law. Under international law, sovereign states are all considered equal, and no state can interfere with the internal affairs of another sovereign state. As a result, the value and authority of international law is dependent upon the voluntary participation of states in its formulation, observance, and enforcement.

5. **The correct answer is (B) FALSE.** While Article 2(7) of the UN Charter explicitly recognizes the sovereignty of states, and in general there is a principle of non-interference in the domestic affairs of sovereign states, the Security Council's Article VII powers clearly contemplate the use of force against a state when necessary to restore peace. And, the recently clarified Responsibility to Protect (R2P) authorizes the United Nations to take action to avert a humanitarian catastrophe within a state when that state's government cannot or will not act.

6. **The correct answer is (E).** All of the criteria listed are requirements of statehood. These criteria come from Article 1 of the Montevideo Convention on the Rights and Duties of States, which was signed in 1933 and came into effect in 1934. The Convention, which pre-dates the United Nations, specifies that only states shall be deemed persons under international law.

7. **The correct answer is (A) TRUE.** So long as the entity satisfies the criteria in the Montevideo Convention, it is a state, even if it is not a member of the United Nations. During the Cold War, certain states (like North and South Vietnam) were excluded from the United Nations for political reasons, even though they satisfied the criteria of statehood.

8. **The correct answer is (B) FALSE.** Under the declarative theory of statehood, a state's existence is independent of recognition by other states. By contrast, the constitutive theory of statehood ties existence as a state to recognition by other states. The case of Taiwan is a good example of how the two theories can occasionally conflict. Taiwan satisfies all of the Article 1 criteria from the Montevideo Convention and thus under the declarative theory of statehood would be considered a state. However, because of political tensions with China, few states recognize Taiwan. Therefore, under the constitutive theory of statehood, there is a good argument that Taiwan is not a state. In the context of state dissolution and/or colonialism, these doctrines have obvious implications.

9. **The correct answer is (B).** Under the declarative theory of statehood, an entity becomes a state as soon as it satisfies the criteria listed in the Montevideo Convention which includes: a defined territory, a permanent population, a government, and the capacity to enter relations with other states. It is possible, albeit unlikely, that Sealand satisfies those criteria. If so, it would be a state under the declarative theory of statehood. However, to be a state under the constitutive theory of statehood, an entity must be recognized as such by other states. Since the facts say that no other state recognizes Sealand, it would not be a state under the constitutive theory of international law. Although Sealand would be the smallest state on record, size alone would not prevent statehood under either theory. Therefore, **Answer (A) is incorrect.** UN membership is not a pre-condition for statehood, so **Answer (C) is incorrect.** While international law recognizes a right to self-determination, that right exists largely in the context of decolonization and does not give all groups the right to form states whenever and wherever they wish. Therefore, **Answer (D) is incorrect.** Conquest is not a pre-condition of statehood and under current international law is no longer considered a legitimate way to establish sovereignty over territory. Therefore, **Answer (E) is incorrect.**

10. **The correct answer is (E).** The term public international law embraces a wide variety of legal regimes governing the conduct and relationships between states, between states and international organizations, and between those entities and persons both natural and legal. Public international law certainly comprehends the relations between states. For example, public international law defines the criteria for statehood, and establishes states as the principal actors in the international legal system. However, public international law also governs the outer bounds of permissible treatment of individuals by states with comprehensive public international law regimes dealing with human rights, prisoners of war, and refugees. Therefore, **Answer (D) is incomplete and incorrect.** Answer (C) is similarly incomplete. The UN Charter is an important part of public international law, and is the foundation for much public international law governing the use of force, arms control, the pacific settlement of disputes and other important functions of the maintenance of international peace and security. However, public international law encompasses much more than just the UN Charter, or the laws governing use of force. For example, public international law also governs many issues relating to the global environment, like climate change, international waters, Antarctica and outer space. Therefore, **Answer (C) is incorrect.** Because public international law does not include the domestic law of states,

Answer (A) is incorrect. The choice of law when there are conflicts in the domestic laws of different states relating to a private transaction is often called "private international law," therefore, **Answer (B) is incorrect.**

11. **The correct answer is (B).** Private International law is a body of law that governs choice of law (or conflicts of law) when there is an international dimension to a private dispute. For example, when a contract dispute arises between parties who are citizens of different states, private international law offers a set of rules that can be used to determine which state's legal system, and laws should govern the resolution of the dispute. Because private international law involves the resolution of conflicts between the domestic law of states, rather than the substance of that law per se, **Answer (A) is incorrect.** The UN Charter is a vital part of public international law, but is not generally considered to play a similar role for private international law, therefore, **Answer (C) is incorrect.** Similarly, the relations between states is an important topic in public international law, but typically is only tangentially related to private international law, which focuses on resolving disputes arising from conflict of laws governing private disputes. Therefore **Answer (D) is incorrect.** **Answer (E) is incorrect** because it is the definition of public international law, not private international law.

12. **The correct answer is (C).** International law's binding force is based on the consent of states. That consent can be either express or implied. International law does not depend on the existence of police powers. Therefore, **Answers (B) and (D), which posit some form of police power, are incorrect.** Nor does international law's binding force stem from judicial oversight. Therefore, **Answer (A) is incorrect.** This lack of police power and judicial oversight means that international law derives its binding force from the consent of states. This marks a big distinction between international law and the domestic law of a state. The major exception to the consent-based model of international law is the Security Council's authority under Chapter VII of the UN Charter to take military and non-military action "to restore international peace and security." However, most of the Security Council's deliberations, activities and resolutions do not implicate that power. For the most part, there is no way to compel states to comply with decisions of the Security Council, the General Assembly and the ICJ. Nonetheless, states regularly invoke these sources of international law in their diplomatic relations, negotiations and policymaking.

13. **The correct answer is (C).** International law does not have a centralized legislature, nor does it have a court with compulsory jurisdiction or an executive with enforcement powers. Therefore **all of the other answers, which posit that international law has at least one of those attributes, are incorrect.** Indeed, this lack of overarching control structure, and in particular, the lack of enforcement power has led some to question whether international law is "really" law at all.

14. **The correct answer is (B) FALSE.** National courts and tribunals decide many, and probably the majority of disputes that arise under international law. For example, *Medellin v. Texas*, 552 U.S. 491(2008), involved a dispute about the proper implementation of the United States' duties under the Vienna Convention on Consular Relations, and the proper treatment to be accorded to a previous International Court of Justice decision in the same dispute.

15. A treaty can bind a state not party to the treaty when: (1) the treaty codifies customary

international law; or (2) when the treaty has become customary law or represents an obligation *erga omnes*. For example, the Vienna Convention on the Law of Treaties is widely described as codifying customary law concerning treaties. By contrast, many of the provisions of the Law of the Sea Treaty are now accepted, even by non-parties like the United States, as customary international law. The Treaty on the Peaceful Use of Outer Space has been deemed to create obligations that every state owes to other states.

16. Article 2.2 of the UN Charter requires that all member states fulfill their duties under the Charter in good faith. Article 26 of the Vienna Convention on the Law of Treaties similarly requires that states fulfill their duties under treaties in good faith. Article 31(1) of the Vienna Convention extends that duty of good faith to treaty interpretation.

17. **The correct answer is (B).** *Lex ferenda* means "law as it should be'" The term is often juxtaposed with *lex lata*, which means "law as it is." Therefore, **Answer (A), which offers the definition of *lex lata*, is incorrect.** The other answers have nothing to do with the definition of *lex ferenda* and are incorrect. The chief importance of the terms *les ferenda* and *lex lata* is in analyzing the appropriate level of influence to accord to the "teachings of the most highly qualified publicists," a subsidiary source of international law under Art. 38(1) of the ICJ Statute.

18. **The correct answer is (A).** An obligation *erga omnes* creates non-derogable duties for all states. In the Barcelona Traction Case, (Second Phase) the ICJ pointed out that states hold certain obligations *erga omnes*, or for all the world. These obligations include upholding *jus cogens* norms like the ban on piracy, genocide, slavery and torture, as well as certain treaty provisions that have been deemed to create obligations for all states. Because, as used in international law, the phrase obligations *erga omnes*, focuses on obligations that states owe each other, **Answers (C) and (E), which focus on individual obligations are incorrect.** Because obligations *erga omnes* exist independent of a state's status as a UN member, **Answers (B) and (D) are incorrect.**

19. **The correct answer is (C).** Soft law refers to non-binding and/or quasi-legal instruments. Included within the rubric of soft law are the many international law codes of conduct, statements, and principles that are often very influential in shaping behavior, their quasi-legal status notwithstanding. The work of NGOs can and often does create this kind of quasi-legal soft law instrument, but NGOs are not the only, or even primary, source of soft law. For example, General Assembly resolutions are also considered soft law. Therefore, **Answer (D) is incomplete and incorrect.** Contracts are almost never binding on non-parties. That aspect of contract law does not convert a contract that would be enforceable under state law into a soft-law agreement. Therefore, **Answer (B) is incorrect.** UN treaties are intended to be hard law. While a treaty that has not yet come into force may be treated as soft-law in the interim, it would be a rare use of the term soft law, and certainly does not constitute the vast majority of soft law. Therefore, **Answer (A) is incorrect.**

20. Soft law can "harden" into hard law either by widespread acceptance through the practice of states, which results in soft law attaining the status of customary law, or by express incorporation into the body of a treaty.

21. **The correct answer is (B).** Article 53 of the Vienna Convention on the Law of Treaties define *jus cogens norms*, also called preemptory or non-derogable norms, as those that are

"accepted and recognized by the international community of states as a whole as a norm from which no derogation is permitted and which can be modified only by a subsequent international norm of the same character." That means that even states objecting to the norm are bound by it, and any treaty conflicting with a *jus cogens* norm is void. Among the norms most often mentioned as *jus cogens* are the international prohibitions on genocide, slavery, torture and piracy. **All of the other answers are incorrect** because they identify social norms that are widely recognized as important for a just society, but are not viewed as non-derogable on the international level.

22. **The correct answer is (E).** All of the answers in this question are part of the monist theory of international law, which asserts that international and domestic law are part of a single legal system, with international law as the ultimate source of all legal authority. Under this theory, states make domestic law through the exercise of power delegated to them under international law. As a result, when international and domestic law conflicts, international law will trump domestic law.

23. **The correct answer is (A).** A dualist theory of international law views domestic and interntional law as separate, equally-important legal systems. If there is a conflict between domestic and international law obligations, whichever obligation arose later in time will prevail. Under a dualist an approach, compliance with a later-adopted state law does not relase the state from its international obligation in the event that international law is incompatible with a latter-adopted state law. The state may thus be in compliance with state law although in violation of international law. Therefore, **Answers (C) and (D), which posit a simple hierarchical relationship between domestic and international law are incorrect. Answer (B) is nonsensical and obviously incorrect.**

24. **The correct answer is (C).** IGOs are associations of states established by a treaty to pursue the common aims of their member states. Also called Intergovernmental Organizations, an IGO has a legal personality separate from its member states, and can enter into legally binding agreements with other IGOs or with other states. The United Nations, the North Atlantic Treaty Alliance (NATO) and the Organization of American States are examples of international governmental organizations. Because IGOs involve states, **Answers (A) and (B) are incorrect.** While a few IGOs include NGOs or sub-state entities as non-voting members (for example the Arctic Council includes indigenous groups as participants) and even more grant those groups observer status, IGOs are primarily *inter-governmental*, meaning they are about states. Therefore, **Answer (D) is incorrect.**

25. **The correct answer is (B) FALSE.** The Council of Europe is a model of intergovernmental cooperation. By contrast, the European Union is a supra-national cooperation model. Unlike the European Union, the Council of Europe has no law-making power (with the exception of human rights where the European Convention gives the European Court of Justice binding legal jurisdiction.) Proposals from the Council of Europe are binding on state parties only if the states accept or otherwise ratify those proposals. The European Union, by contrast, promulgates laws that are binding on all member states.

26. **The correct answer is (E).** Under the modern view, the subjects of international law are not only states and intergovernmental organizations like the United Nations, but under certain circumstances, such as crimes against humanity, can also include individuals. The traditional view was that only states were subjects of international law. With the founding of the United

Nations, that view expanded to include intergovernmental organizations. *See* Advisory Opinion on Reparations for Injuries Suffered in the Service of the United Nations, 1949 I.C.J. 174 (Apr. 11). More recently, developments in international humanitarian and human rights law make it clear that there are circumstances under which individuals can have both rights and obligations under international law. *See* LeGrand Case (Ger. V. U.S.) 2001 I.C.J. 466, 497, par 77 (June 27).

27. **The correct answer is (B) FALSE.** Article 1(2) of the UN Charter identifies friendly relations between states based on the principles of self-determination and equality as a purpose of the United Nations, and paragraph 1(2) of the International Covenant on Civil and Political Rights declares that all peoples have the right to self-determination. However, if this principle is taken to its logical conclusion, it would create significant tension with the international law principles of the territorial integrity of states and *uti possidetis*. Thus, the definition of "peoples," to whom this right of self-determination applies is fairly restrictive. Despite arguments on the part of indigenous groups and separatist groups within states, the principle of self-determination has been limited largely to former overseas (so-called "bluewater") colonies. That is not to say that international law absolutely prohibits secession, but that it is very difficult to get other States, which always have concerns about their own secessionist-minded populations, to recognize a secession if the State concerned opposes it.

28. **The correct answer is (D).** The principle of *uti possidetis* maintains the consistency of international borders when former colonies achieve independence. This principle has caused a great deal of difficulty in Africa and other areas where former Colonists drew political boundaries that did not match the traditional political or ethnic divisions. Because *uti possidetis* has to do with decolonization not secession, **Answers (A) and (B) are incorrect.** **Answer (C) states the opposite of the doctrine of *uti possidetis* and is therefore incorrect. Answer (E) is incorrect** because it is not the role of the United Nations to ratify borders. However, in cases of dispute over the proper border between states, many states have referred these questions to the ICJ for peaceful settlement.

29. **The correct answer is (B) FALSE.** Even though a State and its territory are usually considered to be interchangable, a State is a legal construct that acts through its government. A change in the government of a State, even a violent one, does not affect the legal personality of the State itself. Thus a State that has suffered an overthrow of its government is still bound by the treaties to which it is a party. However, its new government may not be recognized as the rightful government of the State, and may therefore be limited it its ability to act on behalf of the State in international settings.

30. **The correct answer is (C).** Both the United States, as the flag state, and Jon's Shipping, as the vessel owner would have a cause of action. There would be an international dispute between the United States and Canada over the treatment of the vessel because the right to innocent passage by merchant ships and the obligation to permit the exercise of that right, are rights and obligations that rest with states. This cause of action could be brought before an international tribunal, or in the courts of either state. Jon's shipping could not bring a cause of action before an international tribunal. However, Jon's Shipping could bring a cause of action in domestic court asserting that seizure of the ship constituted a violation of international law. For this reason, **Answers (A) and (B) are incomplete**, and **Answer (D) is incorrect. Answer (E) is incorrect** because part of the justification for the international law principle of innocent passage is to protect international peace and security — the actual

circumstances of a particular seizure are not relevant.

31.   The term American Exceptionalism was coined by German Marxists in the 1920s. Focusing on the abundant natural resources of the United States, the term was intended to be an explanation for why the United States was not experiencing the level of class conflict that existed in Europe. However, the idea of American Exceptionalism dates back much farther, to de Toqueville's observations of the United States. He wrote about the special character of the United States as a uniquely free nation based on democratic ideals and personal liberty (even though his observations were made during the time of Cherokee removal, and slavery). In international law, the term "American Exceptionalism" is often used to refer to the United States' position as *the* superpower, and the distance the United States keeps from international law and international institutions. In the context of the Iraq war, there was much discussion of American Exceptionalism and the United States' willingness either to reshape or to ignore international institutions and international law principles like the *jus cogens* prohibition on torture and the UN Charter's prohibition of aggressive war.

32.   **The correct answer is (A).** Under Article 34(1) of the ICJ statute, only States may apply to and appear before the International Court of Justice. The other answers are incorrect because international organizations, other collectivities and private persons are not entitled to institute proceedings before the Court. The African Union is a supranational entity and thus cannot bring a case to the ICJ. Therefore, **Answer (B) is incorrect**. Ulan Bator, a sub-national entity — the capitol of Mongolia, and the Red Cross, an international non-governmental organization, albeit one with special status under the Geneva Conventions, do not have standing to bring contested cases before the ICJ. Therefore, **Answers (C) and (E) are incorrect**. As an organ of the UN, the IMO has the ability under Article 65(1) of the ICJ statute to seek advisory opinions from the ICJ but cannot bring a contested action. Therefore, **Answer (D) is incorrect**.

33.   **The correct answer is (E).** Under Article 96 of the Charter of the United Nations, and Article 65 of the ICJ statute, the ICJ may give advisory opinions on "any legal question" at the request of the UN General Assembly. Therefore, **Answer (D) is incorrect**. Only organs of the UN and those specialized UN agencies authorized by the General Assembly have standing under Article 65(1) of the ICJ statute to request advisory opinions. The General Assembly thus has authority to request an advisory decision. Article 96, paragraph 2 of the United Nations Charter provides that "[o]ther organs of the United Nations and specialized agencies, which may at any time be so authorized by the General Assembly, may also request advisory opinions of the Court on legal questions arising within the scope of their activities." The WHO is a specialized agency authorized by the General Assembly and therefore would have standing to request an advisory opinion, and did so in the *Legality of Threat or Use of Nuclear Weapons*, Advisory Opinion, ICJ Reports (1996) 110 ILR 163, 266. Therefore, **Answer (C) is incorrect**. Greenpeace is an NGO. As such it does not have standing to seek an advisory opinion from the ICJ. The United States is a state and thus has standing to bring contested cases to the ICJ, but not to request advisory opinions. The procedure in advisory proceedings has its origins in the Permanent Court of International Justice, which was authorized to give advisory opinions by Article 14 of the Covenant of the League of Nations.

34.   **The correct answer is (C).** The Rome Statute of the International Criminal Court, which created the ICC, came into force in 2002. Article 25 of the Rome Statute limits the court's jurisdiction to natural persons. Therefore, juridical persons like corporations cannot be tried by the ICC, even if they are accused of crimes that fall within the ICC's purview. Therefore, **Answer (B) is incorrect**. Article 5 of the Rome Statute limits the court's jurisdiction to the most serious crimes under international law, which include crimes against humanity, war crimes, genocide and aggression. As a result, the ICC will not hear cases involving any other crimes. Therefore, **Answers (A) and (D) are incorrect**. Moreover, under the principle of complementarity in Article 17 of the Rome Statute, the ICC's jurisdiction is limited to cases

in which state courts cannot or will not exercise jurisdiction.

35.   **The correct answer is (B) FALSE.** All members of the UN are automatically parties to the ICJ statute. Article 93(2) of the UN Charter allows states that are not members of the United Nations to become parties to the ICJ on a case-by-case basis. Such determinations are made by the General Assembly on the recommendation of the Security Council. However, jurisdiction over a particular dispute depends on the kind of dispute (contentious or advisory) and the consent of the states involved.

36.   Article 31 of the Vienna Convention on the Law of Treaties, which codified customary law on this point, requires that a treaty be interpreted: a) in good faith; b) in accordance with the ordinary meaning of the terms in their context; and c) in light of the object and purpose of the treaty. The language of the treaty forms the primary basis for interpretation, but the treaty's preparatory work and the circumstances of the treaty's conclusions can be supplementary sources of information. The ICJ described this process in *Territorial Dispute (Libyan Arab Jamahiriya v. Chad)* [1994] I. C. J. Reports, Judgment, pp. 21-22, para. 41.

37.   **The correct answer is (B).** Article 36 of the Statute of the International Court of Justice, (ICJ) which is annexed to the Charter of the United Nations, specifies the jurisdiction of the court. Under Article 34, only states may be parties to cases before the ICJ, though under Article 65, the ICJ may give advisory opinions at the request of various UN bodies to the extent that the UN Charter gives them that power. Article 36 specifies that the jurisdiction of the ICJ includes all cases that parties to the ICJ statute refer to the court, and all matters committed to the court's jurisdiction by the UN Charter or treaties that have come into force. Because not all international law matters fall into those categories, **Answer (A) is incorrect.** Because the ICJ's jurisdiction requires state consent, not Security Council consent, **Answer (C) is incorrect. Answer (D) misstates the relationship between international law and domestic law and is therefore incorrect.**

38.   **The correct answer is (C).** The ICJ was established by the United Nations Charter. It is the principle judicial organ of the United Nations. It began work in 1946, the same year that the Permanent Court of International Justice (PCIJ), which had been created by Article 14 of the Covenant of the League of Nations and Article 415 of the Treaty of Versailles ending World War I, was dissolved. Therefore, **Answers (A), (B), (D) and (E) are incorrect.** The ICJ was based closely on the PCIJ, with Article 92 of the UN Charter directing that the ICJ "shall function in accordance with the annexed statute, which is based upon the Statute for the Permanent Court of International Justice." The ICJ statute makes multiple references to the PCIJ statute, and the terms of jurisdiction are very similar. The ICJ has frequently cited decisions of the PCIJ as precedent, and in the *Military and Paramilitary Activities in and against Nicaragua Case*, the ICJ stated that "the primary concern of those who drafted the statute of the present court was to maintain the greatest possible continuity between it and its predecessor."

39.   **The correct answer is (E).** Article 36 of the ICJ Statute specifies all of the choices contained in this answer as the bases upon which the ICJ may have jurisdiction to resolve a dispute between states. Without the consent of the state, however, the ICJ has no jurisdiction.

40.   **The correct answer is (D).** The ICJ has jurisdiction in a contentious case between state

parties that consent to jurisdiction so long as the case involves an issue within the ICJ's competence, as specified in Article 36 of the ICJ Statute. There is no express statute of limitations for bringing cases before the ICJ. Therefore, **Answer (C) is incorrect**.

41.   **The correct answer is (E).** The possible issues listed in this question are all decisions that under Article 36(2) of the ICJ statute, the ICJ may make when it is properly seized of a case. For example, Article I of the European Convention specifically lists these four kinds of questions as those member states commit to refer to the ICJ when disputes arise between members of the European Union.

42.   **The correct answer is (A) TRUE.** Article 4(1) of the Articles on Responsibility of States for Internationally Wrongful Acts specifically include actions of the executive, judiciary and legislature among the acts that can give rise to state responsibility under international law.

43.   **The correct answer is (E).** Under international and domestic law, the United States is bound by decisions of the ICJ, but there are complicated political overlays to this relationship. The UN Charter only specifies that states are bound by ICJ decisions to which they are parties. The Supremacy Clause of the United States Constitution (Art. VI, cl.2) provides that treaties, together with the Constitution and statutes are the "supreme law of the land." At the same time, the Constitution also tasks the Supreme Court with resolving cases and controversies that arise under the laws of the United States (which includes treaties). These contradictory impulses came to a head in an ongoing dispute between the ICJ and the United States over the United States failure to implement a provision of the Vienna Convention on Consular Relations. In *Medellin v. Dretke*, 125 S. Ct. 2088 (2005) President George W. Bush issued a Memorandum recognizing that the United States had an obligation under international law to comply with decisions of the ICJ. This Memorandum was in response to the ICJ's decision in *Avena and other Mexican Nationals (Mexico v. United States)*, 2004. I.C.J. 128, ordering the United States to comply with the Vienna Convention on Consular Relations. However, the memorandum also declared that "the President may decide that the United States will not comply with an ICJ decision and direct a United States veto of any proposed Security Council enforcement measure." It is difficult to see how this Memorandum can be reconciled with the Supremacy Clause of the United States Constitution, other than to state that the President may choose to violate international law.

44. **The correct answer is (C).** The two main ways that international law is created is through agreements (which can include treaties, conventions and other kinds of express agreements) and practice (which is usually referred to as custom). General Assembly resolutions do not carry the force of law. Nor do international conferences. Therefore, **Answer (B) is incorrect.** Chapter VII of the UN Charter gives the Security Council the power to identify threats to international peace and security, and to authorize responses, including the use of force. Security Council resolutions adopted under Chapter VII are binding on UN members and are therefore a source of international law. However, Security Council resolutions adopted under Chapter VI of the UN Charter are not binding. Therefore, **Answer (D) is incorrect.** Art. 38(1)(d) of the ICJ Statute also identifies judicial decisions and the writings of the most highly qualified publicists as a subsidiary source for international law, the vast majority of international law is created through either agreement or practice. Therefore, **Answer (A) is incorrect.**

45. **The correct answer is (D).** Article 38(1) of the 1946 Statute of the International Court of Justice (ICJ) is generally recognized as the definitive statement of the sources of international law. Article 38(1) identifies: treaties, customary law, general principles of law recognized by civilized nations and the writings of the most highly qualified publicists as sources of international law. By contrast, the United States constitution is a key source of national law within the United States, but is not a source of international law (except to the extent the US Constitution represents either customary law, or general principles of law accepted by civilized nations.)

46. **The correct answer is (A).** *Opinio Juris* means "opinion of law." The term is used in international law to signify state practices and actions taken under the belief that such actions and practices are legal obligations. *Opinio Juris* is also referred to as customary law. The opinions of jurists and eminent thinkers are a subsidiary source of international law under Article 38(1) of the ICJ statute. Therefore, **Answer (B) is incorrect.** The term law of war, or *jus in bello*, overlaps to some degree with *opinio juris* but refers to a very specific body of international law composed of customary and treaty-based law. Therefore, **Answer (C) is incorrect. Answer (D) is obviously incorrect** as *opinio juris* refers to a body of law, not to a group of jurists.

47. **The correct answer is (D).** In order for a rule to be considered customary international law, states must habitually act in a manner consistent with the rule. Moreover, states must do this in the belief that compliance with the rule is a matter of law. When both conditions are met, a rule is considered customary law and is binding upon all states. Because customary international law need not be codified in a treaty, **Answer (C) is incorrect.**

48. **The correct answer is (B) FALSE.** In the 1969 *North Sea Continental Shelf* cases, the ICJ stated that treaties are "one of the recognized methods by which new rules of customary

international law may be formed." *North Sea Continental Shelf* (F.R.G. v. Den., F.R.G. v. Neth.), 1969 I.C.J. 3, 41 ¶ 71 (Feb. 20). For example, in the *Fisheries Jurisdiction* case of 1974, the ICJ used international agreements to demonstrate a widespread acceptance of the preferential rights of fishing. *Fisheries* (U.K. v. Nor.), 1951 I.C.J. 116, 138 (Dec. 18). If a treaty, or any portion thereof, becomes customary law, it will bind all states that are not persistent objectors.

49. **The correct answer is (B).** Customary law is created by general adoption of the practice by states. Once a principle becomes customary international law, it is binding on all states, except those that persistently object to the principle. Therefore, **Answer (C), which posits an affirmative action of states is incorrect**. In the *Anglo-Norwegian Fisheries* case, for example, the ICJ stated that the customary international law rule in question was "inapplicable as against Norway inasmuch as she has always opposed any attempt to apply it to the Norwegian coast." *Fisheries* (U.K. v. Nor.), 1951 I.C.J. 116, 131 (Dec. 18, 1951). Judge Lachs made a similar point in his dissention opinion in the *North Sea Continental Shelf* cases. Therefore, **Answer (A) is incorrect**. However, a dissenting state must make its dissent known while the law is still in the state of development. Restatement (Third) of the Foreign Relations Law of the United States, § 102 cmt. d (1987). A state that fails to object during the formation of a rule of customary law will be bound by the rule, even if that state later attempts to object. New states are bound by customary law from the moment of their formation, therefore **Answer (D) is incorrect**. Because customary law binds states and not litigants (except when they are asserting claims that are somehow resolved under international law) and certainly has nothing to do with federal court, as opposed to another venue, **Answer (E) is incorrect**.

50. **The correct answer is (A) TRUE.** General principles of law recognized by civilized nations are used to fill the gaps in international law, particularly in areas of procedure and judicial administration. These general principles include concepts like equity, laches and estoppel. These principles can be found in the decisions of international and domestic tribunals, as well as in state law and the writings of eminent scholars of law. They are propositions that are so fundamental that they will be found in virtually every legal system. Obviously, the terminology "recognized by civilized nations" is outdated.

51. **The correct answer is (D).** The Permanent Court of International Justice found that restitution for an injury, or damages, is a general principle of law, and thus part of international law in the *Chorzow Factory Case*, (Germany v. Poland) 1928 PCIJ Series A No. 17. Equity was similarly recognized as a general principle of law in *Diversion of Water from the River Meuse* (Netherlands v. Belgium) 1937 PCIJ A/B, No. 68 (opinion of Judge Manley O. Hudson.) International law has not embraced trial by jury, which remains a unique feature of common law systems, rather than being a shared feature of civil law and common law systems. Therefore, **Answers (C) and (E) are incorrect**.

52. When treaties and customary international law do not offer a needed international rule, there is a gap or *lacunae* in international law. In order to fill the gap, international tribunals may conduct a comparative law analysis to discover if national legal systems employ a common legal principle to resolve that gap. If such a common legal principle is found across domestic legal systems, then it is presumed that the principle should also be employed to fill the gap in international law.

53. A treaty is a formal written agreement, by which the parties assume or recognize obligations towards each other. Although treaties are typically between states, under international law, intergovernmental organizations also have the capacity to enter into treaties. The Agreement between the United Nations and the United States of America Regarding the Headquartering of the United Nations, (31 Oct. 1947) is an example of a treaty between the UN and a state. Treaties can also be called agreements, protocols, conventions, or covenants. Treaties are often drafted as a single document, but need not be. Treaties can be bilateral or multilateral.

54. A multilateral treaty is a treaty that has more than two states as parties. Each party in a multilateral treaty owes the same obligations to all state parties, except to the extent those specific duties are limited or revised by treaty reservations. Examples of multilateral treaties include the Framework Convention on Climate Change and the United Nations Convention on the Law of the Sea.

55. **The correct answer is (B) FALSE.** Article 2 of the Vienna Convention on the Law of Treaties defines a treaty as "an international agreement concluded between States in written form and governed by international law, whether embodied in a single instrument or in two or more related instruments and whatever its particular designation." Treaties must therefore be in writing.

56. **The correct answer is (C).** Article 2 of the Vienna Convention on the Law of Treaties defines a treaty as an agreement between States. Therefore, **Answer (B) is incorrect**. Under customary law, a treaty is also between States, therefore **Answer (A) is incorrect**. Because the agreement is not between States, reducing it to writing will not affect the status of the agreement and **Answer (D) is incorrect** (and there is no specific consideration requirement for treaties). The General Assembly cannot convert an agreement between a state and an NGO into a treaty, nor is General Assembly ratification required for an agreement to be a treaty, therefore **Answer (E) is incorrect**. The fact that the agreement has no status under international law does not mean that the agreement is not a valid one, or that it cannot be enforced under Russian law.

57. **The correct answer is (C).** A treaty enters into force when it has received the requisite number of ratifications, and satisfied any other conditions specified in the treaty itself. Therefore, **Answer (A) is incomplete and incorrect**. A treaty itself specifies the number of ratifications required for the treaty to come into effect, and that number will vary between treaties. Therefore, **Answer (B) is incorrect**. A treaty can sometimes take a very long time to enter into force. For example, the Law of the Sea Convention was negotiated from 1973 to 1982 when it was opened for signature. The Convention did not come into force until 1994, a year after it received its 60th ratification. Because approval of the United Nations has nothing to do with an international treaty coming into effect, **Answers (D) and (E) are incorrect**.

58. **The correct answer is (A).** Article 2(1)(d) of the Vienna Convention on the Law of Treaties defines a reservation as a unilateral statement, however phrased or named, made by a State when signing, ratifying, accepting, approving or acceding to a treaty whereby it purports to exclude or to modify the legal effect of certain provisions of the treaty in their application to that State. **Answers (C), and (D) which contemplate multi-lateral action are therefore incorrect**. Answer (B), which posits a unilateral commitment to join a treaty regime, is a

very different kind of unilateral commitment than that described in Article 2(1)(d) and **Answer (B) is therefore incorrect**. A valid reservation does limit the scope of a treaty, vis-à-vis the reserving state. Therefore, **Answer (E) is incorrect**.

59. **The correct answer is (D).** The reservation is invalid and Spain remains a party to the treaty. Article 19(c) of the Vienna Convention on the Law of Treaties provides that a state may not file a reservation to a treaty that violates the object and purpose of that treaty. Therefore, **Answer (C) is incorrect**. Article 19(c) also provides that a State filing such a reservation remains a party to the treaty and its invalid reservation simply drops out of its acceptance. Therefore, **Answers (A) and (B) are incorrect**. Nothing in the UN Charter authorizes the use of force under these circumstances, so **Answer (E) is incorrect**.

60. **The correct answer is (A) TRUE.** Article 21 of the Vienna Convention on the Law of Treaties allows states to negotiate reservations that modify how reciprocal treaty obligations will apply in the relations between those states. Such reservations do not apply to other members of the treaty, and are subject to the requirement in Article 19(c) that the reservations not violate the object and purpose of the treaty.

61. **The correct answer is (B).** A treaty is self-executing when it is directly applicable and enforceable in a domestic legal system without further legislative or executive action. Whether or not a treaty is self-executing has nothing to do with the number of states that ratify the treaty. Therefore, **Answer (A) is incorrect**. The language of a treaty, not an act of the President, determines whether a treaty is self-executing, and no Presidential proclamation can convert a non-self-executing treaty into a self-executing one. Therefore, **Answer (D) is incorrect**. Different states have different standards for when a treaty is considered self-executing. In the United States, a treaty is self-executing when there is no need for implementing legislation before it creates specific rights and/or duties. Therefore, **Answer (C) is incorrect** because it states the opposite of a self-executing treaty. Whether or not a treaty creates an individual right of action has nothing to do with whether or not a treaty is self-executing. Therefore, **Answer (E) is incorrect**.

62. **The correct answer is (B) FALSE.** Although many treaties do not create individual rights, it is possible for them to do so. For more than a century, the United States Supreme Court has recognized that treaties can create individual rights, that can be enforced in domestic courts. *Head Money Cases*, 112 U.S. 580, 598-99 (1884). The ICJ has similarly recognized that treaties can create individual rights enforceable in state domestic courts. *Avena and other Mexican Nationals (Mexico v. United States)*, 2004 I.C.J. 128.

63. **The correct answer is (E).** The UN Charter authorizes the use of force in very narrow circumstances, and the breach of obligations under a treaty is not one of them (with the possible exception of the Genocide convention and particular provisions of the Geneva Conventions which might trigger a Responsibility to Protect — for more on this topic, see questions in chapter 5, and 6 on the use of force and humanitarian law). Therefore, **Answers (A) and (B) are incorrect**. A breach of a treaty obligation, even a material breach, does not invalidate the treaty, nor does it provide a justification for all other parties to cease complying with the treaty obligation. Therefore, **Answers (C) and (D) are incorrect**. With the exception of the Geneva Conventions, a breach by one party *does* furnish a directly affected party with the option to cease complying with that treaty obligation.

64.   **The correct answer is (B) FALSE.** Under international law, treaties can be referred to by many different names, and calling something an executive agreement does not change the binding status of such an agreement under international law. However under United States domestic law, there is a significant difference between a treaty and an executive agreement because only a treaty requires the advice and consent of the Senate.

65.   **The correct answer is (E).** Article 1 of the UN Charter identifies maintaining international peace and security, respecting equal rights and self-determination of peoples, and promoting respect for human rights as purposes of the United Nations. Article 1's emphasis on cooperation, read with Article 2's specific recognition of the sovereign equality of states and the limits on intervention into the domestic affairs of states makes it clear that the UN Charter is not an attempt at world government. Therefore, **Answer (A) is incorrect**.

66.   **The correct answer is (A).** The League of Nations was founded by the Treaty of Versailles, which ended World War I as a vehicle for international cooperation. The League ceased to exist after its final meeting in 1946, at which time it transferred its assets to the newly-formed United Nations. Therefore, the other answers to this question, which describe the League of Nations as a subsidiary entity within the United Nations, or the European Union are incorrect. Under Articles 8-11 of the Covenant of the League of Nations, member states committed themselves to preventing war through collective security, disarmament, and settling international disputes through negotiation and arbitration.

67.   **The correct answer is (B) FALSE.** Article 2(7) of the UN Charter prohibits the United Nations from intervening in matters that are "essentially within the domestic jurisdiction" of any state. The only exception is actions authorized by the Security Council under Chapter VII of the UN Charter to keep international peace and security.

68.   **The correct answer is (B) FALSE.** Article 103 of the UN Charter provides that if there is a conflict between obligations under the UN Charter and obligations under any other international agreement, the UN Charter obligations take precedence.

69.   **The correct answer is (B).** Article 7 of the UN Charter establishes: the General Assembly, the Security Council, the Economic and Social Council, the Trusteeship Council, the International Court of Justice and the Secretariat as the principle organs of the United Nations. The Human Rights Council is a subsidiary body of the General Assembly. It was created in 2006 as the successor to the Human Rights Commission.

70.   **The correct answer is (A).** The Trusteeship Council is an organ of the United Nations, not an organ of the European Union. The primary organs of the European Union are the European Commission, the Council of Ministers, the European Parliament and the European Court of Justice. The European Commission is in many ways the heart of the European Union. It is a civil service that acts as a guardian of the treaty, formally originates all legislative measures and is responsible for the implementation of all directives and other decisions of the Council of Ministers. The Council of Ministers is the ultimate decision-making body in the Union. There are, in fact, many 'Councils' consisting of ministers from member states with specific portfolios - such as agriculture, transport and social affairs. No directive can be issued, or amended, unless it is agreed by the Council. The Council must

also approve all regulations issued to interpret or apply Directives. The European Parliament is composed of elected representatives of each member state. It has the power to approve the president and members of the European Commission. The Parliament is a forum for discussion, and can comment and suggest amendments to legislation proposed by the European Commission. The European Court of Justice is the judicial body tasked with interpreting the directives and regulations adopted by the Council. It is not the same thing as the European Court of Human Rights.

71.   **The Correct answer is (C).** Under Article 39 of the UN Charter, the Security Council has primary responsibility for the maintenance of international peace and security. The General Assembly can be a forum for discussing issues related to international peace and security but does not have primary responsibility for their maintenance. Therefore, **Answer (A) is incorrect**. The ICJ can contribute to the peaceful resolution of disputes, but is not charged with maintaining international peace and security. Therefore, **Answer (B) is incorrect**. The Secretary General's Office of Peacekeeping is one of the tools that the Security Council has at its disposal in order to maintain peace and security. However, the Office of Peacekeeping can only act with Security Council authority. Therefore, **Answer (D) is incorrect**. The Trusteeship Council was focused on decolonization, not on maintaining peace and security (though dissatisfaction with colonial rule was obviously a source of upheaval that threatened peace and security.) Therefore, **Answer (E) is incorrect**.

72.   **The correct answer is (D).** Under Article 39 of the UN Charter, the Security Council is specifically authorized to respond to threats to peace, breaches of the peace and to acts of aggression.

73.   **The correct answer is (A) TRUE.** When the Security Council has determined under Article 39 that a threat to peace exists, Article 42 gives the Security Council authority to take "such action by air, sea, or land forces as may be necessary to maintain or restore international peace and security."

74.   **The correct answer is (A) TRUE.** When the Security Council has determined under Article 39 that a threat to peace exists, Article 41 gives the Security Council the authority to completely or partially interrupt economic relations, as well as to embargo rail, sea, and air travel; block postal, telegraphic, radio, and other communications; and to sever diplomatic relations.

75.   **The correct answer is (A).** Under Article 23 of the UN Charter, the Security Council is composed of 5 permanent members and 10 non-permanent rotating members. The permanent members are: the United States, United Kingdom, France, China, and the Russian Federation. The non-permanent members are chosen by regional groups and elected by the General Assembly for two-year terms.

76.   **The correct answer is (C).** Even though Germany and Japan are important world economic and political powers, they were defeated during World War II. When the United Nations was formed in the wake of World War II, the Security Council was constructed to give veto powers to the victorious allied countries: the United States, Russia, France, Great Britain, and China. France is the only country on the list of possible answers that was among the World War II allies. Therefore, **Answers (A), (B), and (D) are incorrect**. That said, India and Brazil are important emerging powers, both economically and politically. Were the

Security Council to be reformed today, they would be likely candidates for permanent seats. Indeed, one of the criticisms of the Security Council is that its membership does not reflect actual world power. One of the more dramatic moments in the history of membership of the Security Council was the General Assembly's 1971 decision to award China's seat on the Security Council to the People's Republic of China, thereby stripping the Republic of China (Taiwan) of the seat that both entities claimed.

77. **The correct answer is (D).** Under Article 27(3) of the UN Charter, a Security Council resolution must receive nine affirmative votes, including the concurring votes of all five permanent members. Thus a negative vote by any of the permanent members will be sufficient to prevent the adoption of any non-procedural resolution. The permanent members are therefore said to have veto power.

78. **The correct answer is (E).** Critiques of the Security Council typically focus on the disproportionate influence that the veto power gives to the permanent members. The ability of a single permanent member to thwart the will of the rest of the international community gives rise to criticism about a lack of democratic accountability. While during the tenure of John Bolton as the United States representative at the United Nations there were complaints about a lack of civility, the workings of the Security Council, even when very contentious, typically maintain a façade of cordiality (they do call it diplomacy, after all.)

79. The Responsibility to Protect (R2P) is a framework for using the existing tools of international law (e.g., mediation, early warning mechanisms, economic sanctioning, and Chapter VI powers) to prevent mass atrocities. R2P focuses on preventing genocide, war crimes, crimes against humanity and ethnic cleansing. It consists of three principles: 1) States have the primary responsibility to protect their populations from mass atrocities; 2) the international community has an obligation to provide assistance to States in building capacity to protect their populations from mass atrocities; and 3) the international community has a responsibility to take timely and decisive action to prevent and halt mass atrocities when a State is manifestly failing to protect its populations. R2P was announced as part of the Outcome Document of the 2005 World Summit. It was subsequently ratified by the Security Council (S/RES/1674) and by the General Assembly (A/RES/63/308).

80. **The correct answer is (B) FALSE.** The Responsibility to Protect has become a new norm of international law, but is not a *jus cogens* norm (at least not yet). Were it a *jus cogens* norm, there could be no derogation from R2P.

81. **The correct answer is (A).** Under Article 97 of the UN Charter, the Secretary General is the United Nations' chief administrator. Although the Department of Peacekeeping Operations is part of the United Nations Secretariat, and peacekeeping operations are under the responsibility of an Under-Secretary General, there is no UN army. Therefore, **Answer (B) is incorrect**. Although Article 99 of the UN Charter gives the Secretary General the authority to refer questions to the Security Council, the Secretary General is not the chair of the Security Council. Therefore, **Answer (C) is incorrect**. Nor is the Secretary General the chair of the General Assembly. Therefore, **Answer (D) is incorrect**. Indeed, under Article 98 of the UN Charter the Secretary General deals with matters referred to his/her office by the Security Council, as well as the General Assembly and other UN organs.

82. **The correct answer is (D).** Under Article 9 of the UN Charter, all member states have the

right to be represented in the General Assembly, and under Article 18 all member states have one vote in the General Assembly. By contrast, all of the other organs have membership that is limited in some fashion by the UN Charter, making the other answers incorrect. Article 23 of the UN Charter provides that the Security Council shall have 15 members — five permanent and 10 that rotate among the general membership. Therefore, **Answer (A) is incorrect**. Article 61 of the UN Charter specifies that the Economic and Social Council shall have 54 members elected from the general membership. Therefore, **Answer (C) is incorrect**. Article 86 describes the complicated formula for electing and appointing the members of the Trusteeship Council. Article 92 of the UN Charter specifies that the International Court of Justice will be administered according to the ICJ statute, which provides in Article 3 that the Court will consist of 15 members elected by the General Assembly. Therefore, **Answer (B) is incorrect**. Article 97 of the UN Charter specifies that the Secretariat is composed of a Secretary General and his/her staff. Therefore, **Answer (E) is incorrect**.

83. **The correct answer is (B) FALSE.** The General Assembly does not have the power to adopt binding international law, only the Security Council has that power within the United Nations. General Assembly resolutions are therefore considered "soft law" even though some of them have been very influential in shaping international law.

84. **The correct answer is (B) FALSE.** Under Article 108 of the UN Charter, the Charter can only be amended by two-thirds vote of the General Assembly that is then ratified by two-thirds of the member states, including all the permanent members of the Security Council.

85. **The correct answer is (E).** The International Labor Organization (ILO) is a specialized agency within the United Nations. It is responsible for drawing up and overseeing international labor standards. The ILO brings together representatives of governments, employers and workers to jointly shape policies intended to promote decent working conditions. This 'tripartite' structure makes the ILO unique among United Nation institutions.

86. **The correct answer is (B) FALSE.** Just war theory, which dates back to St. Augustine, focuses on the intent or purpose behind the use of force. The theory would allow a state to wage war as a response to another state's unjust actions. The actions typically cited include avenging wrongs inflicted by the state or its subjects, or responding to unjust seizures. Just war theory explicitly rejects the use of force without justifying circumstances.

87. **The correct answer is (B).** Under modern international law, conquest is no longer a legitimate means for acquiring title to territory. Therefore, the decision to annex Cancun would be illegal regardless of the motivations that prompted the invasion, and **Answer (A) is incorrect**. Had the US merely invaded and not annexed any territory, it might possibly have been able to justify its actions by invoking the right to self-defense (it would obviously depend on the surrounding circumstances). But because the United States annexed territory, **Answer (C) is incorrect**. As recently as the 19th Century, conquest was viewed as a legitimate instrument of foreign policy, but that is no longer the case. Therefore, invasion to resolve a drug smuggling problem would not be legal and **Answer (D) is incorrect**.

88. **The correct answer is (B) FALSE.** Under Article 2(4) of the UN Charter, states are directed to refrain from "the threat or use of force against the territorial integrity or political independence of any state, or in any other manner inconsistent with the Purposes of the United Nations." However, Article 51 explicitly recognizes the inherent right of self-defense. Moreover, under Article 42, the Security Council has the power to authorize the use of force. Even the Kellogg-Briand Pact, which purported to outlaw the use of force before the Second World War allowed for self-defense.

89. **The correct answer is (B).** *Jus ad bellum* means the law governing the right to use force. Key provisions of the UN Charter (Articles 2(4), 43 and 51) articulate a framework for the legitimate use of force under international law. The law applicable during wartime is known as *jus in bello*. Therefore, **Answer (A) is incorrect**. The UN Charter's framework for *jus ad bellum* marks a break with pre-World War I international law which focused primarily on *jus in bello*. There is no special law governing the enforcement of peace treaties, therefore **Answer (C) is incorrect**.

90. **The correct answer is (A) TRUE.** In the Nicaragua Case, the International Court of Justice recognized the principle of the non-use of force as customary international law. *See Military and Paramilitary Activities in and Against Nicaragua (Nicaragua v. United States),* Merits, 1986 I.C.J. 14. Therefore, even if a state is not bound by the UN Charter, it is still bound by the *jus in bellum* principles articulated therein.

91. **The correct answer is (B) FALSE.** Article 53 of the UN Charter recognizes an inherent right of individual or collective self-defense. NATO is an example of a collective self-defense organization. Under Article 5 of the North Atlantic Treaty, the NATO parties agree that an

armed attack on one treaty partner shall be considered an attack against all, thereby triggering an obligation on the part of NATO parties to assist the attacked state.

92. **The correct answer is (E).** International law contemplates the use of force under two circumstances: as self-defense under Article 51, and as authorized by the Security Council under Article 42. The United States argued that under Article 51, it had an inherent right to self-defense that included anticipatory self-defense, and that prior Security Council resolutions authorized the use of force against Iraq. Both arguments were extremely controversial at the time, and remain so to this day. There is no inherent right of conquest, and the international community no longer recognizes conquest as a means of acquiring title to territory. Indeed Article 2(4) of the UN Charter would seem to reject the use of force for such a purpose. Therefore, **Answer (C) is incorrect.**

93. **The correct answer is (A).** The Mine Ban Treaty was adopted in just 14 months, and the International Campaign to Ban Landmines, led by American Jody Williams, played a key role in the drafting and adoption of the treaty. The treaty was drafted largely outside traditional diplomatic channels, and the International Campaign had a formal seat at the table during all negotiations. Their contribution, along with the International Committee of the Red Cross is acknowledged in the Preamble to the Treaty and the two organizations shared the 1997 Nobel Peace Prize for their efforts. The Treaty has nothing to do with the Security Council, so **Answer (B) is incorrect.** The Treaty has wide participation (167 states as of this writing) but is far from universal. Among the states not parties to the Convention are the United States, China, and many Middle-Eastern countries. Therefore, **Answer (C) is incorrect.** Other treaties that ban specific weapons include the Geneva Protocol banning poisonous and asphyxiating gases; the Convention on Biological Weapons; the Convention on Chemical Weapons; and the 1899 Hague Convention which banned expanding bullets. Therefore, **Answer (D) is incorrect.**

94. **The correct answer is (D).** International humanitarian law includes *jus ad bellum* (the law governing the permissibility of going to war) and *jus in bello* (the law applicable during war.) It thus deals with the protection of individuals during armed conflict. There are humanitarian law provisions concerning civilians, combatants, and prisoners of war. The Geneva Conventions of 1949 and their two Additional Protocols form the core of international humanitarian law. Aside from the UN Charter, the Geneva Conventions are among the most widely ratified international agreements. As of this writing, there are 194 parties to the Geneva Conventions. The Optional protocols of 1977 have also been widely adopted, with 170 parties to Optional Protocol I and 165 parties to Optional Protocol II. However, humanitarian law does not address the terms of peace treaties, so **Answer (C) is incorrect.**

95. **The correct answer is (B) FALSE.** Even if a state resorts unlawfully to the use of force, international humanitarian law will still apply to all parties involved in the conflict. The preamble to the Geneva Convention Additional Protocol I of 1977 lays out this obligation very clearly. Moreover, much of international humanitarian law contained in the Geneva Conventions has become customary law, and therefore would apply to all states, even those not party to the Geneva Conventions.

96. **The correct answer is (C).** This independence of obligations under international humanitarian law makes the international humanitarian law treaties and the obligations they create somewhat different from other treaties. For these obligations, compliance is not dependent on corresponding compliance by others but is required in all circumstances. Thus, if one party violates international human rights law during a conflict, (for example by killing POWs) other parties to the conflict are not entitled to retaliate in kind, or to otherwise respond by themselves breaching international humanitarian law. While acts of reprisal are not completely forbidden by international law, reprisals cannot involve acts that are *malum in se*, like violating human rights, or breaching international humanitarian law or *jus cogens* norms.

97. **The correct answer is (A) TRUE.** There is no requirement of a formal declaration of war before international humanitarian law applies to a conflict. Common Article 2 of the four Geneva Conventions makes it clear that humanitarian law applies not only to declared wars but also to all other armed conflicts.

98. **The correct answer is (E).** The Geneva Conventions and their two Additional Protocols form the core of international humanitarian law. There are four Geneva Conventions that, along with two optional protocols are collectively referred to as the Geneva Convention. The first Geneva Convention addresses the treatment of sick and wounded field soldiers. The Second Geneva Convention addresses the treatment of sick and wounded sailors. The third Geneva Convention addresses the treatment of prisoners of war. The fourth Geneva Convention addresses the treatment of civilians during conflict.

99.   **The correct answer is (B) FALSE.** Common Article 3 of the Geneva Convention explicitly identifies international humanitarian law obligations that bind states during conflicts that are not of an international character. Wholly intrastate conflicts would thus be covered at a minimum by Common Article 3.

100.   **The correct answer is (B) FALSE.** It is certainly true that armed conflicts between a state and a non-state actor like a terrorist group do not fit neatly into the Geneva Convention categories of international armed conflict between states, or internal armed conflict between a state and an insurgent group. However, in the wake of the Iraq War, the United States Supreme Court was faced with precisely this question. In *Hamden v. Rumsfeld*, 126 S.Ct. 2749 (2006), the Supreme Court ruled that Common Article 3 applied to the conflict between the United States and Al Qaeda. Since the United States was the primary proponent of the notion that the Geneva Convention did not apply to such conflicts, it is safe to say that international law is now relatively clear on this point.

101.   **The correct answer is (E).** Common Article 3 requires the parties to the conflict to treat all non-combatants humanely (including civilians, POWs or others *hors de combat* by sickness or wounds). Torture, hostage taking, cruel, degrading or humiliating treatment are all prohibited. When the United States Supreme Court declared in *Hamden v. Rumsfeld*, 126 S. Ct. 2749 (2006) that the United States was bound by Common Article 3 in its ongoing conflict with Al Qaeda, one of the major consequences was that the ruling invalidated the military commissions created by President Bush, which were not regularly constituted courts, and are thus prohibited by Common Article 3.

102.   **The correct answer is (A) TRUE.** In the *Tadić* case, the International Criminal Tribunal for Yugoslavia (ICTY) ruled that it had jurisdiction over Article 3 crimes. *Decision of Appeals Chamber in Tadić (Jurisdiction) Case* IT-94-I-72, 105 ILR 453, 489. The International Criminal Tribunal for Rwanda (ICTR) also asserted expansive jurisdiction over Article 3. Article 8(2) of the Rome Statute gives the International Criminal Court jurisdiction over crimes committed during internal armed conflicts in addition to international conflicts. Therefore, crimes under Common Article 3 are expressly within the jurisdiction of the International Criminal Court.

103.   **The correct answer is (E).** All of these obligations are laid out in the Geneva Conventions in great detail.

104.   **The correct answer is (B) FALSE.** The term Hague law refers to the laws governing how hostilities may be conducted. The term Geneva law refers to the treatment of non-combatants. There are obvious overlaps between the requirements that fall under each of the two terms, and as international humanitarian law develops and matures, their use is gradually falling out of favor.

105.   **The correct answer is (E).** A basic principle of international humanitarian law is that "the right of belligerents to adopt means of injuring the enemy is not unlimited." Hague Convention IV, Art. 22. The Hague Declaration of 1899 banned the use of expanding bullets; the use of such munitions is identified in Article 8(2)(b) of the Statute of the International Criminal Court as a war crime. The Geneva Protocol of 1925 prohibits the use of asphyxiation and poisonous gases, as well as other chemical or biological weapons. The 1972 Biological Weapons Convention and the 1993 Chemical Weapons Convention extended the

Geneva Protocol's prohibitions to include the development, production or transfer of such weapons.

106. **The correct answer is (C).** In an advisory opinion, the ICJ held unanimously that international humanitarian law applies to the threat or use of nuclear weapons. *Legality of Threat or Use of Nuclear Weapons*, Advisory Opinion, ICJ Reports (1996) 110 ILR 163, 266. Therefore, **Answer (E) is incorrect**. In that same decision, by a very close vote, the ICJ opted not to conclude whether the threat or use of nuclear weapons would be lawful in an extreme circumstance of self-defense when the very survival of the state is at stake. Therefore, **Answers (A), (B) and (D) are incorrect** because they state positive conclusions about a question that remains open under international law.

107. **The correct answer is (A).** The principle of proportionality means that belligerents must not launch an attack when the anticipated death and injury to civilians is clearly excessive in light of the military advantage expected from the attack. Additional Protocol I, Art. 51(5); and Rome Statute 8(2)(b)(iv). Under international humanitarian law, the death of civilians is not, in itself a war crime, so **Answer (B) is incorrect. Answer (C) is incorrect** because it is the articulation of a different principle of international humanitarian law — the principle of distinction — which makes an attack directed at civilian targets a war crime in its own right. Additional Protocol I, Art. 51(2); and Rome Statute 8(2)(b)(i). **Answer (D) is incorrect** because it has nothing to do with international law and is factually incorrect.

108. **The correct answer is (E).** All four Geneva Conventions identify willful killing, torture, willfully causing serious injury and extensive destruction or appropriation of property as grave breaches of the Geneva Convention. Many of these actions would also amount to war crimes under the Rome Statute.

109. **The correct answer is (B) FALSE.** For grave breaches of the Geneva Conventions, states are obligated to establish and exercise universal jurisdiction. Article 49 of the First Geneva Convention, Article 50 of the Second Geneva Convention, Article 129 of the Third Geneva Convention and Article 146 of the Fourth Geneva Convention all contain identical language obligating parties to search for alleged violators, regardless of their nationality or place of offense, and to either try violators before their own courts or to hand them over to another party for trial. This principle of universal jurisdiction is rooted in the belief that grave breaches of the Geneva Convention are such serious crimes that all states have a responsibility to bring those responsible to justice. In order to fulfill this responsibility, the vast majority of countries have enacted universal jurisdiction laws that enable their national criminal justice system to investigate and prosecute persons suspected of committing these crimes, and to ensure that their country is not used as a "safe haven" to evade justice.

110. **The correct answer is (B) FALSE.** The International Court of Justice addressed this question after a Belgian arrest warrant was issued for the then Minister of Foreign Affairs for the Democratic People's Republic of Congo. The warrant had been issued as a purported exercise of universal jurisdiction for alleged war crimes and crimes against humanity. *Arrest Warrant of 11 April 2000 (Democratic Republic of the Congo v. Belgium)*. The ICJ concluded that State officials had immunity under international law while serving in office. Therefore, State officials enjoy immunity from arrest in another State on criminal charges, including charges of war crimes or crimes against humanity. However, the ICJ did indicate that State officers "may be subject to criminal proceedings before certain international

criminal courts." And, various international law cases, most notably the Pinochet case, the Charles Taylor Case before the Special Court for Sierra Leone, and the Milosevic trial before the ICTY make it clear that former heads of state can be subject to prosecution for acts that occurred while they were heads of state.

111. **The correct answer is (A) TRUE.** The International Committee of the Red Cross (ICRC) is specifically named in all four 1949 Geneva Conventions. Under the Geneva Conventions, ICRC's primary responsibility with regard to prisoners of war is to make visits to prison camps, assess conditions there, call for improvements where necessary, and make reports to prison authorities of their findings. This role as the principal humanitarian organization named in the Geneva Conventions makes the ICRC unique among non-governmental organizations.

112. **The correct answer is (D).** The Martens clause, which is part of the Preamble to the 1899 Hague Convention II — Laws and Customs of War on Land, states in relevant part that "populations and belligerents remain under the protection and empire of the principles of international law, as they result from the usages established between civilized nations, from the laws of humanity, and the requirements of the public conscience." The clause was named in honor of Fyodor Martens, the Russian delegate at the Hague Peace Conference of 1899, and the clause's language was based on a speech that Martens gave to the assembled delegates. Because it directly contradicts the text of the Martens clause, **Answer (A) is incorrect. Answer (B) is a true statement**, but is wholly unrelated to the Martens clause. **Answer (C) is also wholly unrelated to the Martens clause**.

113. **The correct answer is (E).** The various options offered for answering this question are taken from the titles of the four Geneva Conventions.

114. **The correct answer is (C).** Humanitarian intervention was NATO's justification for its intervention in the Federal Republic of Yugoslavia. In 1999, NATO forces mounted a bombing campaign against Serbia in an attempt to stop the attacks on civilians in Kosovo and prevent a humanitarian catastrophe. China and Russia had vetoed a Security Council resolution that would have authorized this use of force, therefore **Answer (E) is incorrect.** Although the legal justification for this kind of humanitarian intervention (meaning action without the authorization of the Security Council) remains extremely controversial, particularly after the United States claim that its invasion of Iraq qualified as a humanitarian intervention, there is a general consensus that intervention to stop genocide or other serious violations of international law does not violate Article 2(4) of the UN Charter. Therefore, **Answer (B) is incorrect. Answer (A) is incorrect** because the League of Nations Charter said nothing about humanitarian intervention and had no provisions that could be interpreted as dealing with the concept. **Answer (D) is incorrect.**Even though there are some rough parallels between the claims that European colonization benefitted the colonized lands and humanitarian intervention; humanitarian intervention is focused on averting an immediate crisis, and cannot involve any attempt to claim sovereignty over the lands and peoples involved.

115.   **The correct answer is (D).** The International Criminal Court has jurisdiction over genocide and other systematic crimes carried out as official policy during war. Article 5 of the Rome Statute specifically limits the jurisdiction of the ICC to genocide, crimes against humanity, war crimes and the to-be-defined crime of aggression. Because the court does not have jurisdiction over human rights abuses unrelated to these crimes, or abuses committed by legal rather than natural persons, **Answer (B) is incorrect.** The ICC has no jurisdiction over ordinary crimes like fraud or smuggling, even when those crimes have an international dimension. Therefore, **Answer (A) is incorrect.** Answer (C) misstates the relationship between the ICC and domestic courts — the ICC does not oversee convictions in national courts. Indeed, the ICC's jurisdiction over the crimes listed in Article 5 is complimentary, meaning that the ICC has jurisdiction only when national courts cannot or will not try those accused of violating Article 5.

116.   **The correct answer is (E).** Article 5 of the Rome Statute, which created the International Criminal Court, identifies genocide, war crimes, crimes against humanity and aggression as the crimes within the court's jurisdiction.

117.   Article 6 of the Rome Statute defines genocide to be any of a list of enumerated acts when committed with the intent to destroy, in whole or in part, a national, ethnic, racial or religious group. The enumerated acts are: killing members of the group; causing serious bodily or mental harm to members of the group; deliberately inflicting on the group conditions of life calculated to bring about its physical destruction in whole or in part; imposing measures intended to prevent births within the group; and forcibly transferring children of the group to another group.

118.   **The correct answer is (B) FALSE.** Article 39 of the UN Charter includes aggression in the list of acts that trigger the Security Council's authority to take actions under Articles 41 and 42 to restore the peace. There is no accepted definition of aggression, however. Article 5(1)(d) of the Rome Statute gives the ICC jurisdiction over aggression but Article 5(2) stipulates that the Court may not exercise jurisdiction over the crime of aggression until the state parties agree on a definition for the crime. Efforts to define the crime are ongoing.

119.   Article 7 of the Rome Statute defines crimes against humanity to be any of a list of enumerated acts when committed as part of a widespread or systematic attack directed against any civilian population. The enumerated list includes: murder; enslavement; deportation or forcible transfer of a population; torture; rape, sexual slavery, enforced prostitution, forced pregnancy, enforced sterilization, or any other form of sexual violence of comparable gravity; as well as other inhumane acts of a similar character intentionally causing great suffering, or serious injury to body or to mental or physical health.

120.   Article 8 of the Rome Statute defines war crimes to be either grave breaches of the Geneva

Conventions, or other serious violations of the international law of armed conflict (*jus in bello*). Among the enumerated grave breaches of the Geneva Conventions are: willful killing, torture or inhuman treatment, willfully causing great suffering or serious injury to body or health, and extensive destruction and appropriation of property not justified by military necessity and carried out unlawfully and wantonly. Among the enumerated serious violations of the international law of armed conflict are: intentionally attacking civilians or civilian installations, intentionally attacking humanitarian workers or peacekeepers, intentionally attacking undefended civilian targets that have little or no military objective, and killing or wounding combatants after they have surrendered.

121. **The correct answer is (B) FALSE.** Under the principle of complementarity, the International Criminal Court is a court of last resort rather than the first court to be seized of jurisdiction. Therefore, under Article 17 of the Rome Statute, the ICC may not exercise jurisdiction, even if the crimes alleged otherwise fall within the ICC's jurisdiction whenever a case is being investigated or prosecuted by a State with jurisdiction. If a case has been investigated by a State with jurisdiction, and the State has decided not to prosecute, the ICC will not have jurisdiction unless the decision resulted from an unwillingness or inability of the State to genuinely prosecute. If the person concerned has already been tried for conduct that is subject to a complaint before the ICC, Article 20(3) of the Rome Statute prohibits the ICC from exercising jurisdiction unless the earlier proceedings were conducted for the purpose of shielding the individual from liability, or were not conducted according to international norms of due process.

122. The principle of complementarity refers to the idea that the ICC will supplement, rather than supplant State jurisdiction over the crimes enumerated in Article 5 of the Rome Statute. The Preamble and Article 1 of the Rome Statute make it clear that the ICC has jurisdiction that is complementary to national criminal jurisdiction and is intended to supplement and support state investigations and prosecutions. As such, complementarity is often considered to be the cornerstone of the Rome Statute and the ICC.

123. **The correct answer is (B) FALSE.** The ICC is not an organ of the United Nations, although there is a close relationship between the two institutions. Pursuant to Article 2 of the Rome Statute, which directs the ICC to establish a relationship with the UN, the President of the ICC and the UN Secretary General negotiated a Relationship Agreement in 2004. This agreement established a framework for cooperation between the two institutions while also affirming the independence of the Court. Among other provisions, this Agreement allows participation of the ICC, in the capacity of observer, in the UN General Assembly; it also facilitates the exchange of information between the two institutions and establishes an obligation to consult on matters of mutual interest. In addition to the Article 2 requirement that the ICC establish a relationship with the UN, there are other provisions in the Rome Statute that spell out aspects of the relationship. Under Article 13(b) of the Rome Statute, the UN Security Council, when exercising its Chapter VII power, may refer situations to the Prosecutor when one or more of the crimes listed in Article 5 may have been committed. The Security Council used this authority in 2005 when it referred the situation in Darfur to the ICC prosecutor (Security Council Res. 1593/2005). Under Article 16 of the Rome Statute, the Security Council may defer the commencement or continuation of 'an investigation' or 'a prosecution' by the ICC prosecutor for a renewable period of 12 months.

124. **The correct answer is (C).** Under Article 25(1) the ICC has jurisdiction over natural

persons. Although there was a lengthy discussion during the drafting period, the Rome Statute does not give the Court jurisdiction over legal persons.

125. **The correct answer is (E).** Under Article 25(3) of the Rome Statute individuals who: commit a listed crime, either singly or jointly, as well as individuals who aid and abet the commission of a listed crime; solicit the commission of a listed crime; or attempt to commit a listed crime can be subject to the jurisdiction of the ICC.

126. **The correct answer is (A) TRUE.** Article 25(3)(e) of the Rome Statute includes incitement to commit genocide as an action triggering the jurisdiction of the ICC. In adopting this position, the Rome Statute follows the Rwanda Media Case decided by the International Criminal Tribunal for Rwanda. *Prosecutor v. Nahimana*, Case No. ICTR 99-52-T, Judgment and Sentence, ¶¶ 5–7 (Dec. 3, 2003).

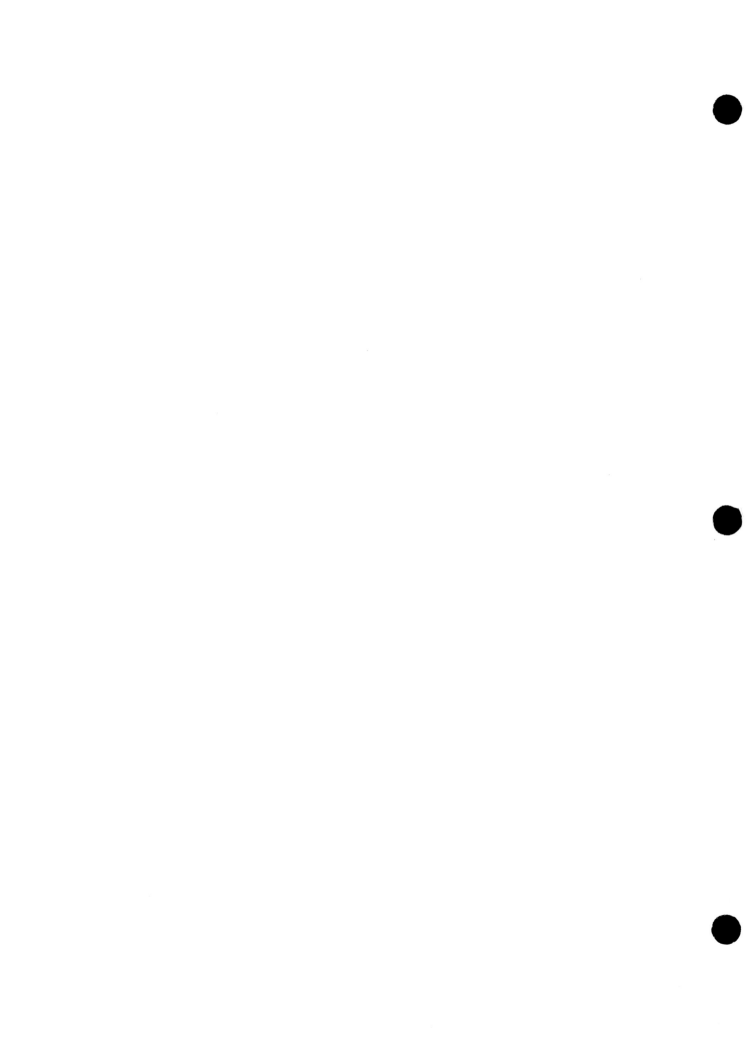

127. **The correct answer is (D)**. International human rights are enforceable. Therefore, **Answer (E) is incorrect**. Enforcement can occur at the domestic, regional or international level. Therefore, **Answer (A) and (B), which claim exclusive jurisdiction over human rights, are incorrect**. By ratifying human rights treaties, states commit themselves to respecting those rights and ensuring that their domestic law is compatible with the treaties and with international human rights norms. Moreover, because the Universal Declaration is considered to be customary law explaining the basic commitments of the UN Charter to human rights, not being a party to a human rights treaty does not necessarily mean that a state has no human rights obligations. Therefore, **Answer (C) is incorrect**. When domestic law fails to provide a remedy for human rights abuses parties may be able to resort to regional or international mechanisms for enforcing human rights. For example, the Inter-American Court of Human Rights has heard many cases alleging human rights violations after domestic courts refused to vindicate those rights.

128. **The correct answer is (C)**. While a primary function of International Human Rights Law is to protect individuals from their own governments, this body of law also includes the law of state responsibility for injury to aliens, which protects individuals from the actions of other governments. Therefore, **Answer (A) is incorrect** because it is too narrow. The many international human rights treaties place obligations on states that may include the obligation to ensure that individuals and non-state actors under their control do not violate human rights, but do not directly place obligations on individuals or non-state actors. Therefore, **Answers (B) and (D) are incorrect** (even though the Universal Declaration declares that the obligations it articulates apply to all "organs of society.") While human rights are certainly discussed quite frequently at the UN General Assembly, such discussions are a by-product of attempts to define and enforce human rights, rather than the purpose of those rights. Therefore, **Answer (E) is incorrect**.

129. **The correct answer is (A) TRUE**. International human rights law, and the law of state responsibility for injury to aliens protects individuals when they are outside of their own country. Together these two bodies of law establish certain minimum standards of treatment to which all human beings are entitled from states.

130. **The correct answer is (B)**. International human rights law emerged as a legal doctrine during World War II. The genocide and other atrocities that occurred during the war forced the international community to recognize that individuals needed protection against their own governments. This was important for international law as a whole because prior to that time, international law was thought of as law between the states. Therefore, **Answer (A) is incorrect**. After World War II and the rise of international human rights law, international law was also conceived of as a law that could regulate matters within states. International human rights law recognized that the treatment of individuals within a state was not solely up to the discretion of that state; it is an international issue. In 1948, the United Nations

General Assembly adopted the Universal Declaration of Human Rights and sponsored the conclusion of the Convention on the Prevention and Punishment of the Crime of Genocide. The other answers, all of which significantly post-date the Universal Declaration are further developments of the concept of human rights articulated in the Universal Declaration. Therefore, **Answers (C), (D), and (E) are incorrect.**

131. **The correct answer is (A) TRUE.** Article 55(c) of the UN Charter provides that the United Nations "shall promote . . . universal respect for, and observance of human rights and fundamental freedoms for all."

132. **The correct answer is (A).** The rule that emerged from *Texas Overseas Petroleum Co. v. Libyan Arab Republic* is that international law, not domestic law, governs questions of expropriation. Therefore, **Answers (B), (C) and (E) are incorrect**. The New York Convention of 1958 governs enforcement of arbitral awards and does not speak to the law that governs disputes over expropriation of property. Therefore, **Answer (D) is incorrect.**

133. **The correct answer is (C).** The law of state responsibility affords protection to corporations and other legal individuals, as well as to individuals. However, international human rights law provides protection only to natural persons. Therefore, **Answer (E), which states the opposite scope of protection, and Answer (A) which asserts that the two doctrines are identical, are incorrect.** There are also differences in the scope of rights protected. For example, property investments and other economic interests of aliens are also protected by the law of state responsibility and not by human rights law. At the same time, the law of state responsibility does not protect people from offenses committed by their own national government, and human rights law does. Therefore, **Answer (D) is incorrect.** Because human rights law also protects non-nationals, **Answer (B) is incorrect.**

134. **The correct answer is (B).** The obligation to treat foreign nationals lawfully was owed to the state of the individual's nationality. The legal fiction that the injury suffered by an alien abroad was an injury to the state of nationality was necessary because historically only states were deemed subject to international law, and individuals did not hold rights under international law. *See Mavrommatis Palestine Concessions* (Jurisdiction) P.C.I.J., Ser. A, No. 2 (1934). As a result, disputed injuries to aliens were commonly resolved through diplomatic negotiations between the governments concerned. Therefore, **Answer (A) is incorrect.** Because the law of State Responsibility does not involve actions by the United Nations High Commissioner or by the Security Council, **Answers (C) and (D) are incorrect.**

135. **The correct answer is (C).** Historically, states relied on the so-called "general principles of law recognized by civilized nations." This source of law was codified in Art. 38(1)(c) of the ICJ Statute. Today, actions based on the doctrine of state responsibility tend to be based on multilateral and bilateral treaties. The Draft Articles were completed in 2001, but have not yet come into force. Even when the Articles do come into effect, they will not eliminate obligations under other treaties or under customary law, so **Answer (E) is incorrect.**

136. **The correct answer is (D).** Before a state can be held responsible for any action, it is necessary to prove that the injury is attributable to an official act or omission, and that the act or omission constitutes a breach of the state's obligations under international law. As non-state actors ranging from transnational corporations, non-governmental organizations

and terror organizations wield more influence in the international arena, and as governments privatize traditional government functions, this limitation on state liability has become a focus of critical international attention. There is no statute of limitations for state responsibility, so **Answer (C) is incorrect**.

137. **The correct answer is (D).** The Universal Declaration is generally considered to be the authoritative interpretation of the United Nations Charter obligation to respect and promote human rights articulated in Article 1(3) of the Charter. And, many eminent scholars and jurists consider the Universal Declaration to be a statement of customary international law. Moreover, a number of General Assembly resolutions refer to the "duty" of states to observe the provisions of the Universal Declaration. The Universal Declaration is not itself a treaty, but has been the basis for most of the international human rights treaties negotiated since 1948. Those treaties are ratified by state parties, not by the General Assembly. Therefore, **Answer (A) is incorrect**.

138. **The correct answer is (C).** Article 2 of the Universal Declaration states that everyone is entitled to the rights set forth in the Declaration, without distinctions of any kind. The Declaration repeatedly uses the word "everyone" in order to emphasize the universality of the rights articulated. Therefore, the other possible answers to this question, which would all limit the rights in some fashion, are incorrect.

139. **The correct answer is (D).** Article 3 of the Universal Declaration provides that everyone has the rights to life, liberty and security of person. Article 6 provides that everyone has the right of recognition as a person before the law. Article 8 provides that everyone has the right to an effective remedy for a violation of the fundamental rights guaranteed by law.

140. **The correct answer is (A).** Article 13(1) of the Universal Declaration provides that everyone has the right to freedom of movement within a state, and Article 13(2) provides that everyone has the right to leave one's country and to return. Therefore, **Answers (B) and (C) are incorrect**. However, the Universal Declaration does not provide that everyone has the right of freedom of movement to pursue one's livelihood. As international economic law has lifted restrictions on global movement of capital, the lack of a comparable right for global movement of labor has become a source of significant contention.

141. **The correct answer is (B) FALSE.** Although there are signs of significant progress in the realization of some rights articulated in the Universal Declaration, at least in some regions of the world, we are still far from the goal of full realization. The various NGO report cards, as well as the United States' State Department Reports on Human Rights continue to identify a litany of fundamental human rights abuses around the world.

142. **The correct answer is (A).** Article 2(1) of the ICCPR requires each state party to undertake "to respect and to ensure to all individuals within its territory and subject to its jurisdiction the rights" enumerated in the Covenant. The obligation is immediate upon ratification. **Answers (B), (C) and (D) are incorrect** because they suggest that implementation need not be immediate. **Answer (E) is incorrect** because the ICCPR is an international agreement that creates binding law obligations for all states that have ratified the treaty.

143. **The correct answer is (B) FALSE.** A major critique of international human rights law is that it over-emphasizes civil and political rights (so-called first generation rights) at the

expense of social and economic rights (so-called second-generation rights) or environmental rights (so-called third generation rights.)

144.   **The correct answer is (B).** Article 2(1) of the ICESCR requires states to "take steps . . . to the maximum of their available resources with a view toward achieving progressively the full realization of the rights recognized in the Covenant." **Answer (A) is incorrect** because the obligations in the ICESCR do not necessarily become binding immediately. **Answers (C) and (D) are incorrect** because they state time lines that are not found in the treaty itself. **Answer (E) is incorrect** because the ICESCR is an international agreement that creates binding law obligations for all states that have ratified the treaty.

145.   **The correct answer is (B) FALSE.** Negative rights focus on limitations of state power vis-à-vis individuals or groups. For example, limits on the state's ability to silence dissent, imprison individuals, discriminate against individuals on the basis of race, creed or gender, or limitations on the state's ability to confiscate property are negative rights. Rights to a basic standard of living, like a right to food or shelter would be positive rights.

146.   **The correct answer is (C).** In particular, indigenous and minority groups argue that more attention to group rights is needed in order to protect their rights collectively and individually. These groups sometimes claim that human rights are unduly biased toward individualist societies and cultures, and therefore work to the detriment of more communal societies. This argument is often made by indigenous groups, and sometimes by representatives of societies found in Africa and Asia. Viewed through this lens, fully implementing human rights, as articulated in the Universal Declaration involves replacing the fundamental values of one civilization with those of another, a form of cultural imperialism reminiscent of the colonial era.

147.   **The correct answer is (B) FALSE.** The ICESCR does not give ECOSOC enforcement authority and there is no procedure for individuals or states to make complaints. Under Article 16 of the ICESCR, states commit to submit periodic reports on the progress made in achieving observance of the rights enumerated in the Convention. Each year, the Committee on Economic, Social and Cultural Rights reports to ECOSOC on the conclusions it has reached from the state reports. ECOSOC serves as a forum for international discussion of issues of social and economic rights.

148.   **The correct answer is (B) FALSE.** The Human Rights Committee, a body of independent experts within the office of the UN High Commissioner for Human Rights can receive complaints from individuals alleging violations of their rights under the ICCPR if the state concerned has ratified the Optional Protocol to the ICCPR. The Council can also receive complaints by one state against another, so long as both have recognized this role of the Council under Article 41 of the ICCPR. To date, no such inter-state complaints have been made. The ICESCR does not have a complaint mechanism.

149.   **The correct answer is (A).** The biggest obstacle to implementation of human rights agreements is the selectivity of states based on their domestic political concerns. The potential beneficiaries of human rights often ally together to press for their implementation so **Answer (B) is incorrect**. In this process, they are often joined by NGOs, which tend to be a strong voice for human rights implementation, in the UN and around the world, so **Answer (C) is incorrect**. There are multiple international NGOs within and without the

United Nations that are devoted to discussing and debating human rights, so **Answer (D) is incorrect**.

150. **The correct answer is (E).** The Human Rights Council was created in 2006 by General Assembly Resolution 60/251. Prior to that time, these functions had been carried out by the Commission on Human Rights. Among its tasks are conducting periodic universal review of states' compliance with the ICCPR, and recommending measures to the General Assembly for the further development of international human rights law. **Answer (B) is incorrect** because the Human Rights Council has no enforcement authority. **Answer (C) is incorrect** because the Human Rights Council is not an adjudicatory body, and has no authority to prosecute human rights violators.

151. **The correct answer is (B) FALSE.** The European Court of Human Rights administers the European Convention for the Protection of Human Rights and Fundamental Freedoms, which was adopted under the auspices of the Council of Europe. This treaty, which has been ratified by 46 states, predates the European Union (it entered into force in 1953). The European Court of Human Rights should not be confused with the European Court of Justice, which is an organ of the European Union. The European Union is not a party to the Convention and plays no role in either the European Court of Human Rights or the European Convention for the Protection of Human Rights.

152. **The correct answer is (B) FALSE.** The regional human rights agreements are intended to be forums of last resort for allegations of human rights abuses. Therefore, Article 46(a) of the American Convention, Article 35(1) of the European Convention and Article 50 of the African Charter all require exhaustion of domestic remedies as a pre-condition for the regional court exercising jurisdiction.

153. **The correct answer is (A) TRUE.** The European Court of Human Rights is part of the Council of Europe, not part of the European Union.

154. **The correct answer is (B) FALSE.** When the European Convention was first adopted, individuals did not have standing to submit cases to the Court. However, Article 34 of Protocol 11 to the European Convention, which entered into force in 1998, gave the Court power to receive applications from any individual, NGO or group claiming to have been the victim of a violation of the European Convention by a State Party.

155. **The correct answer is (E).** Article 32 of the European Convention specifies that the Court shall have jurisdiction over all matters interpreting the Convention. Under Article 1, High Contracting Parties commit to assure the rights guaranteed in the Convention to all persons under the jurisdiction of the Parties. However, jurisdiction is generally interpreted to mean within the territory of the state in question, though lands occupied and controlled by the state may also be included. However, the Convention does not apply to actions of the State outside that territory, nor does it apply to the actions of non-State actors. Therefore, **Answers (A), (B), and (C) are incorrect**. Article 56 allows a State to declare that the provisions of the Convention will apply to territories for whose international relations the State Party is responsible (meaning colonies or territories). Thus, absent such a declaration, the rights and obligations articulated in the Convention do not apply within those territories. Therefore, **Answer (D) is incorrect**.

156.   **The correct answer is (A) TRUE.** The Charter of Fundamental Rights of the European Union, which entered into force with the Treaty of Lisbon in 2009, enshrines a much broader set of rights than does the European Convention on Human Rights. The Charter includes civil, political, social and economic rights for European Union citizens and residents. However, the Charter only applies to EU member states when they are implementing EU law. All members of the EU are also members of the Council of Europe. The European Convention guarantees a narrower set of rights but applies to all Council of Europe members, which includes a number of states that are not members of the European Union, like Turkey.

157.   **The correct answer is (A) TRUE.** The Organization of American States adopted the Declaration of the Rights and Duties of Man, and OAS members have an obligation to promote the rights proclaimed in the Declaration. However, not all member states have ratified the American Convention on Human Rights (notably the United States, Canada and Cuba are not parties) which established the Inter-American Commission on Human Rights and the Inter-American Court of Human Rights. Because the Inter-American Commission on Human Rights oversees both OAS Charter obligations and American Convention obligations, all OAS members must accede to the jurisdiction of the Inter-American Commission. The Inter-American Court, however, only has jurisdiction over the American Convention.

158.   **The correct answer is (D).** As soon as a state has ratified the American Convention, Article 44 gives the Inter-American Commission jurisdiction to consider complaints filed by individuals. However, under Article 45, the Commission has jurisdiction over complaints filed by one state against another only if both states have also accepted the Commission's jurisdiction to receive inter-state applications. The other answers misstate the jurisdiction of the Inter-American Commission and are therefore incorrect.

159.   **The correct answer is (A) TRUE.** The African Charter on Human and Peoples' Rights recognizes not only individual rights, but also group rights. These group rights include the rights of peoples to exist (Art. 20), the equality between peoples and the rejection of domination by one people over another (Art. 19), the right to natural resources (Art. 21) and the right to economic, social, and cultural development (Art. 22).

160.   **The correct answer is (E).** The Millennium Development Goals (MDGs) were adopted by the General Assembly in 2001. They set a target of reaching the 8 Millennium Development Goals by 2015. The answers listed in this question are all targets identified in the Millennium Development Goals. The MDGs provide a framework for the entire UN system, and for the international community, to work coherently together toward a common end.

161.   **The correct answer is (B) FALSE.** There are obvious overlaps between the MDGs and basic human rights, most notably Article 25 of the Universal Declaration which affirms that "[e]veryone has the right to a standard of living adequate for the health and well-being of himself and of his family, including food, clothing, housing and medical care." However, human rights are more comprehensive than the MDGs, protecting more aspects of human existence, and applying universally to all countries (the MDGs focus on developing countries). Human rights are legally binding obligations enshrined in treaties or customary law, while the MDGs are a set of targets that are not legally enforceable. Notwithstanding those differences, many view the MDGs and human rights as interdependent and mutually

enforcing frameworks. The MDGs have galvanized international efforts to realize fundamental social and economic rights.

162.   **The correct answer is (B) FALSE.** ILO Conventions 107 and 169 also address the rights of indigenous peoples, albeit in a less expansive and protective fashion.

163.   Obviously there is a tremendous overlap in fact between peoples that were colonized peoples and peoples that are indigenous peoples. However, under international law, there is a fairly sharp distinction between the two categories — most particularly around the right to self-determination. In fact, prior to the 2007 Declaration, indigenous peoples were typically referred to in international law as indigenous populations in order to drive home that distinction. While there is still much debate over the precise definition of indigenous peoples, ILO Convention 107 limits indigenous populations to those "living within independent states in conformity with the social economic and cultural institutions of another time rather than of the nation to which they belong" and whose ancestors experienced colonization or conquest. Colonized peoples, by contrast, live under the colonial rule of a state located elsewhere. The predominant idea in international law was, for many years, that only peoples under conditions of classical colonization, sometimes referred to as blue-water colonies, were entitled to self-determination. This vision of a colonized people emphasized self-determination in connection with statehood and linked decolonization with self-determination. Thus indigenous peoples living within an already existing state, rather than within a colony controlled by a state located elsewhere, did not qualify as colonized people and were not entitled to self-determination. Or, self-determination was considered the collective right of the entire population of a country — not a right that extended to distinct sub-populations within a state. The 2007 Declaration represents a more nuanced vision of self-determination that emphasizes autonomy rather than statehood.

164.   **The correct answer is (A) TRUE.** Article 7(1) of ILO Convention 107 allows indigenous populations to retain their own customs and institutions but only to the extent they are "not incompatible with the national legal system." The protections described by the 2007 Declaration of Indigenous Rights are much more extensive.

165.   **The correct answer is (D).** The Declaration on Indigenous Rights was adopted by the General Assembly in a vote of 144 in favor, 4 opposed (the United States, Canada, New Zealand and Australia) and 11 abstentions. G.A. Res. 61/295, U.N. Doc. A/RES/61/295 (13 September 2007). The 4 dissenters have subsequently indicated support for the Declaration. While the General Assembly has no authority to create law, under Article 13 of the UN Charter it is charged with encouraging the progressive development of international law. The Declaration certainly represents a major development of international legal norms vis-à-vis indigenous peoples. The Declaration is not a treaty within the definition of the Vienna Convention because a vote in the General Assembly is not the same thing as ratifying a treaty. Therefore, **Answers (A) and (C) are incorrect.** The Declaration is a major step forward from customary international law protections of indigenous people which fall far short of the protections and rights outlined in the Declaration. Therefore, **Answer (B) is**

incorrect. General principles of international law include concepts like laches, due process and equity. The Declaration clearly does not fall into that category, so **Answer (E) is incorrect**.

166. **The correct answer is (B) FALSE.** Article 3 of the United Nations Declaration on the Rights of Indigenous Peoples does affirm that indigenous peoples have the right to self-determination but Article 46(1) narrows that right to the right to self-governance and sovereignty within an existing state.

167. **The correct answer is (B) FALSE.** Article 8j of the Convention on Biological Diversity affirms state sovereignty over natural resources. This recognition of state control is a response to the colonial experience in which natural resources were exploited for the benefit of the colonial masters with little regard for the local consequences. However, because indigenous peoples are often marginalized within states, the Convention on Biological Diversity's affirmation of state control over natural resources does not necessarily protect their interests.

168. **The correct answer is (D).** The Stockholm Declaration, which resulted from the 1972 UN Conference on the Human Environment was the first major international agreement that portrayed environmental issues as global concerns, and also the first to highlight the connection between environmental concerns and development issues. The Declaration raised awareness about the dangers of environmental degradation associated with economic activities and laid a foundation for using international law to control human activities that adversely affected the environment. At the same time, the Declaration tried to reassure newly-independent states of the global South that environmental law was not merely a new way for former colonial powers of the global North to reassert control over their former colonies. To mediate the tension between those two goals, Principle 21 of the Stockholm Declaration recognizes the sovereign right of states to exploit resources pursuant to their own environmental policies, but also declares that states have a responsibility to ensure that activities within their jurisdiction do not cause damage to the environment of other States or the global commons. **Answers (A), (B), and (C) all predate the Stockholm Declaration and are therefore incorrect. Answer (D) is incorrect** because it is fictitious.

169. **The correct answer is (B) FALSE.** International law has already dealt with precisely this question. In the early 20th Century, the Trail Smelter, located in British Columbia near the border with the United States, spewed pollution from a 200 foot smoke stack. Due to prevailing wind patterns, this pollution damaged farmland on the United States side of the United States-Canadian border. Some quirks in the domestic law of both states prevented the injured farmers from seeking restitution in either United States' or Canadian courts. As a result, the dispute over transboundary air pollution became a major political issue. The two countries agreed to refer the dispute to a specially-constituted international arbitration panel. The panel ultimately issued two precedent-setting decisions that articulated the two key principles for resolving disputes over transboudary pollution. First, that states have a responsibility to use their territory in a fashion that does not cause harm outside their territory; and second that the "polluter pays" principle should be the basis for resolving transboundary environmental disputes. These Trail Smelter principles were reflected in Principle 21 of the Stockholm Declaration, and remain key underpinnings of international environmental law. The continued vitality of these principles would give the United States a remedy under international law.

170. **The correct answer is (B).** This concept of intergenerational equity was explicitly incorporated into the 1972 London Ocean Dumping Convention, the 1973 Convention on International Trade in Endangered Species, and the 1972 Convention Concerning the Protection of the World Cultural and Natural Heritage. It was also reflected in the 1986 Brundtland Commission Report, *Our Common Future*, defining sustainable development as "development that meets the needs of the present without compromising the ability of future generations to meet their own needs." Principle 3 of the 1992 Rio Declaration reaffirms this

idea, stating that "[t]he right to development must be fulfilled so as to equitably meet developmental and environmental needs of present and future generations." Negotiations over climate change, persistent organic pollutants and biodiversity all take place against the backdrop created by this principle. However influential it is, the principle of intergenerational equity has not become a *jus cogens* norm from which no derogation is permitted. Therefore, **Answer (A) is incorrect**. The principle of intergenerational equity has very complex ramifications in the human rights context. While the principle is frequently discussed in the context of a human right to health or to a healthy environment, and has obvious implications for many social, cultural and economic rights issues, it has not become a human right on its own. Therefore, **Answer (C) is incorrect**.

171. **The correct answer is (A)**. The race to the bottom is a result of the pressure that global trade places on states to be lower cost producers. Because the cost of environmental damage is rarely included in economic calculations, reduced environmental protection is a way to try to lower the cost of production. The concern is that states will compete to see which one can reduce environmental protection the most in order to attract investment and lower production costs. The regulatory discussion in the wake of BP's Deepwater Horizon spill in the Gulf of Mexico provides an example of how race to the bottom arguments are deployed to stave off or reduce environmental regulation. An oft-repeated argument against the Department of Interior's proposed temporary moratorium on deepwater drilling, and against increased regulation of offshore drilling more generally, was that such regulation in the United States would drive business from the United States toward states with less stringent regulation. **Answer (B) states the opposite of a race to the bottom and is therefore incorrect. Answers (C), (D), and (E) all involve ways to strengthen rather than weaken environmental regulation and are therefore incorrect.**

172. **The correct answer is (C)**. This definition of sustainable development comes from the 1987 report of the World Commission on Environment and Development (widely known as the Bruntland Commission). The report, entitled *Our Common Future*, is generally viewed as the definitive definition of sustainable development. While there are certainly connections between peace and prosperity, this relationship is not the focus of sustainable development. Therefore, **Answer (A) is incorrect**. Tourism, especially eco-tourism can be a component of sustainable development, but sustainable development encompasses much more than tourism. Therefore, **Answer (B) is incorrect**. While one of the effects of embracing sustainable development tends to be an increased role for NGOs and other civil society institutions, that is not the primary aim of sustainable development. Therefore, **Answer (D) is incorrect**.

173. **The correct answer is (A)**. Under Article VII of CITES, each party commits to implementing the convention. Under Article IX, each party commits to having a Management Authority with the power to enforce CITES trade restrictions. Therefore, the most likely scenario is that duly authorized domestic officers are enforcing domestic law that implements CITES. Interpol is an organization dedicated to facilitating police cooperation around the world. It has no independent enforcement powers under international law. Instead, it focuses on pooling and sharing information, facilitating investigations, and developing best practices. Interpol focuses mostly on corruption, terrorism, human and drug trafficking and fugitives. Therefore, **Answer (B) is incorrect**. The Trail Smelter Arbitration dealt with issues of transboundary pollution and its polluter pays and state responsibility

principles are irrelevant to this situation. Therefore, **Answer (C) is incorrect**. TRAFFIC is a very influential NGO that serves as a clearinghouse for information, and often proposes best practices for protecting species listed under CITES. However, it has not been delegated any power to enforce international law, so **Answer (D) is incorrect**. Although the international community might send observers as part of a program to build domestic capacity to enforce CITES within a state, and might even provide enforcement assistance to a state that requested such aid, there is no UN police force and sovereignty concerns dictate that enforcement assistance be provided only at the request of a state. Therefore, **Answer (E) is incorrect**.

174. **The correct answer is (B) FALSE.** The Rio Declaration is soft-law. It is an international statement of principles rather than a binding treaty. Even though the Rio Declaration is not legally binding on states, it is often referred to in international negotiations and/or litigation as an authoritative statement of states' political commitments.

175. **The correct answer is (C).** This statement of the Precautionary Principle comes from Principle 15 of the Rio Declaration and is generally considered to be the definitive statement of the Precautionary Principle under international law. The Precautionary Principle is about how states should make decisions in the face of uncertainty — it does not specify specific substantive outcomes. Nothing in international (or domestic) law requires that actions never harm the environment. Therefore, **Answer (A) is incorrect**. A requirement that states pay damages may flow from the Trail Smelter's polluter pays principle, or from a particular international treaty, but is not part of the Precautionary Principle. Therefore, **Answer (B) is incorrect**. The precautionary principle does not require that states take all available precautions as a precondition of activity. Instead, it prevents uncertainty from being used to prevent precautionary steps. Thus, **Answer (D), which suggests that the Precautionary Principle demands all possible preventive action is incorrect**.

176. **The correct answer is (A) TRUE.** The principle of common but differentiated responsibility contains two basic notions. First, the principle acknowledges the common responsibility that all states share to protect common environmental resources. Second, the principle also promotes a differentiated allocation of those responsibilities based on different historical contributions to global environmental problems, and the disparity of current material, social and economic situations across States. In doing so, the principle acknowledges the legacy of colonialism that left former colonies wary of any interference in their domestic decisionmaking and facing very different development priorities than those generally held by their former colonizers. By acknowledging difference in both the past actions of states and in their current situations, the principle of common but differentiated responsibility establishes a conceptual framework for an equitable allocation of the costs of global environmental protection. It has become a guiding principle of international cooperation.

177. **The correct answer is (B) FALSE.** Interpreting international environmental law requires examining several different treaties, including some that may not immediately seem relevant to the environment. For example, in the MOX Plant Litigation, Ireland claimed that radiation leaks from the British nuclear reprocessing plant at Sellafield England were contaminating the Irish Sea and harming the health of Irish citizens. Ireland initiated proceedings under the Convention on the Preservation of the Marine Environment of the North-West Atlantic (OSPAR) and under the Law of the Sea. Ultimately, the European Court of Justice concluded that it had exclusive jurisdiction over the dispute.

178. **The correct answer is (B).** Framework conventions are frequently used in international environmental law. They are binding legal agreements, so **Answer (C) is incorrect**. These agreements articulate the structure or principles that will then be developed further through detailed annexes, schedules or protocols. Because framework conventions do not specify all the details of implementing the agreement, or even of the agreement itself, **Answer (A) is incorrect**. The Framework Convention on Climate Change and the Convention on Biological Diversity are examples of framework conventions. Although such an agreement might use the law of one jurisdiction as a model, there is no requirement that it do so, therefore **Answer (D) is incorrect**.

179. **The correct answer is (D).** The General Assembly, the Global Environmental Facility and the UN Environmental Programme have all helped develop international environmental law. In 1972, after the UN Conference on the Human Environment, the General Assembly created the UN Environmental Programme (UNEP). Since that time, the General Assembly has regularly weighed in on environmental issues that have proved to be quite influential. Since its founding, the UNEP has mediated the development of environmental treaties, and of international environmental law more generally. The Global Environmental Facility is a partnership between the UN Development Program, the UN Environmental Programme and the World Bank. Its purpose is to help developing countries fund projects that protect the environment.

180. **The correct answer is (E).** In the *Case Concerning Pulp Mills on the River Uruguay (Argentina v. Uruguay)*, the International Court of Justice concluded that that the duty to undertake an EIA when there is a risk of pollution with transboundary elements has achieved customary international law status. **Answer (A) is incorrect** because the Espoo Convention is a treaty adopted by the UN Economic Commission for Europe. Therefore, it does not apply to either Uruguay or Paraguay. **Answer (B) is incorrect** because EIAs are not wholly a matter of domestic law. Aside from the recent ICJ ruling about the status of EIAs as customary law, many international, and bilateral treaties have EIA provisions. **Answer (C) is incorrect** because the Rio Declaration is not legally enforceable. It is a soft-law document that has been tremendously influential, but it does not impose binding obligations on states. **Answer (D) is incorrect** because EIA requirements apply to specific projects or activities rather than to general plans.

181. **The correct answer is (A) TRUE.** Green accounting is a way for states to develop a more complete picture of their overall financial health by including degradation or accumulation of human and natural capital in calculations of GDP. Without this critical adjustment to account for consumption of human and natural capital, GDP numbers may give a deceptive and inaccurate picture of economic progress within a state.

182. **The correct answer is (B) FALSE.** Although human rights treaties do not explicitly protect environmental rights as such, there is a growing sense that environmental rights are key components of the right to life, health and food guaranteed by the International Human Rights Covenants. Moreover, many scholars and jurists are speculating that a number of international environmental law principles, including the right to prior informed consent, access to information and to judicial process may be coalescing into a new human right — the human right to a healthy environment. Cases making these claims have been brought before the Inter-American Court of Human Rights, and the European Court of Human Rights.

183.   **The correct answer is (A).** The IPCC has issued four assessment reports, the most recent in 2007. The assessment reports collect and analyze scientific reports from around the world in order to draw conclusions about the scientific evidence regarding climate change. The IPCC is a scientific organization. It does not draft laws or lobby. Therefore, **Answers (B) and (C) are incorrect.**

184.   **The correct answer is (B) FALSE.** The question poses the exact opposite of the IPCC's actual conclusions. The IPCC concluded that the earth's temperature increases since the mid-20th century are very likely (90-95% certainty) due to observed increases in anthropogenic greenhouse gas emissions. They have also concluded that it is extremely unlikely (less than 5%) that these temperature changes can be explained by natural causes alone.

185.   **The correct answer is (D).** The Millennium Ecosystem Assessment was a United Nations project intended to assess progress toward achieving the goals articulated in the Millennium Development Goals and to document trends in the world's ecosystems. The results were grim. More than a billion people lack access to clean water and/or adequate sanitation. More land was converted to cultivation in the second half of the 20th Century than between 1700 and 1850. Animal species are disappearing at an alarming rate and almost 30% of existing species are endangered or threatened.

186.   **The correct answer is (B) FALSE.** Vessels on the high seas are traditionally viewed as under the jurisdiction of their flag state.

187.   **The correct answer is (C).** In Proclamation No. 2667, entitled *Policy of the United States with Respect to the Natural Resources of the Subsoil and Sea-Bed of the Continental Shelf,* 10 Fed. Reg. 12303 (September 28, 1945) President Truman invoked the customary right of a state to protect and exploit its natural resources. **Answer (A) is incorrect** because *mare liberum* refers to the principles advocated by Dutch theorist Hugo Grotius in his 1609 work *Mare Liberum,* asserting that the sea was international territory that all nations were free to use for seafaring and trade. **Answer (B) is incorrect** because *mare clausum* refers to the principles advocated by Briton John Selden in his 1635 work *Mare Clausum,* that the sea was as capable of national appropriation as was land, and could therefore be brought under the sovereignty of a state. This debate between Grotius and Seldon reflected the differing national positions of the Dutch Republic and England at the time as they competed for domination of world trade. In his 1945 Proclamation, President Truman did not invoke the idea of *mare clausum,* and did not claim sovereignty over the seas themselves.

188.   **The correct answer is (B).** Under UNCLOS Article 55, a state may declare an EES that extends up to 200 nautical miles from its coastal baseline. Overlapping claims are to be resolved either by negotiations between the states themselves or by referring the question to the ICJ. **Answer (A) is incorrect** because the extent of the EEZ has nothing to do with the continental shelf, which may vary widely depending on hydrography. UNCLOS Article 76 controls the criteria by which a state establishes the outer limits of its continental shelf. The coastal state's rights vis-à-vis its EEZ are not the same as the sovereignty rights over the continental shelf laid out in UNCLOS Article 77. **Answer (C) is incorrect** because the 12 nautical mile limit refers to the limit in UNCLOS Article 3 on the extent of the territorial seas over which a state may claim sovereignty. **Answer (D) is incorrect** because the International Seabed Authority, administers resources in the seabed outside the limits of national jurisdiction. It has nothing to do with EEZs. **Answer (E) is incorrect** because it refers to the pre-UNCLOS limits on state claims of sovereignty over adjacent waters. This limit, which was conventionally 3 miles, was thought to be related to the distance that a cannon ball could travel.

189.   **The correct answer is (D).** Although a vessel must be under the jurisdiction of a State and must therefore fly a State's flag, the UNCLOS Article 91 requirement that there be a "genuine link" between the vessel and the flag State is frequently ignored. Some states with very low standards are willing to flag almost any vessel — thereby providing vessels with what is called a "flag of convenience." A flag state is responsible for imposing and enforcing maintenance, operation and financial standards on its vessels. However, when states issues flags of convenience, the actual control that the State has over the vessel is slight. Vessels flying flags of convenience are notorious for violating fishing, pollution and safety standards.

Because a vessel can be flagged by a State to which it has very tenuous connections, **Answers (A) and (B) are incorrect**. Because a vessel is expected to have a nationality and fly a flag, **Answer (C) is incorrect** (Under Article 110(1)(d) vessels suspected of having no nationality, for instance because they fly no flag, can be boarded by the warship of any nation). Under UNCLOS Article 92 vessels are prohibited from flying more than one flag, therefore **Answer (E) is incorrect**.

190. **The correct answer is (A).** Under UNCLOS Article 87, all States enjoy the freedom of the high seas. One consequence is that while each State may exercise jurisdiction over its own vessels, no other State may do so. Under Article 97, only the flag State may arrest or detain a vessel, or exercise criminal jurisdiction over a vessel on the high seas. The only exception to this is that a vessel on the high seas that is suspected of having no nationality may be boarded by a warship of any state under UNCLOS Article 110(1)(d). **Answers (B), (C), and (D), which posit either that a State other than the flag State, or no State may exercise jurisdiction over a flagged vessel are therefore incorrect. Answer (E) is incorrect** because the United Nations has no jurisdiction over vessels on the high seas.

191. **The correct answer is (A) TRUE.** Under UNCLOS Article 3, states may claim sovereignty of up to 12 nautical miles as a territorial sea. However, given the unique character of the sea and its importance to trade, Article 17 of UNCLOS specifies that ships of all states have the right of innocent passage.

192. **The correct answer is (B) FALSE.** Under Article 77(4) of the Law of the Sea Convention, States have sovereign rights, rather than sovereignty over its continental shelf.

193. **The correct answer is (B).** Article 56(1) grants States the power to declare a 200 nautical mile Exclusive Economic Zone (EEZ) in which the State has sovereign rights for purposes of managing, exploiting and conserving natural resources. These resources include living resources like fish, as well as mineral resources found in the sea-bed. One caveat: Australia's ability to control fishing within its EEZ may be limited by regional agreements that Australia may have entered with regard to managing fish stocks. **Answer (A) is incorrect** because the 24-mile limit refers to the contiguous zone described in Article 33 of UNCLOS. The contiguous zone is a 24 nautical mile territory in which a State may exercise the control necessary to enforce its customs, immigration and sanitary laws. **Answer (C) is incorrect** because the 12 mile limit refers to the territorial sea under UNCLOS Article 3. **Answer (D) is incorrect** because there is no correlation between the extent of a state's continental shelf and its EEZ. **Answer (E) is incorrect** because Australia's ability to control fishing extends well beyond its internal waters defined by UNCLOS Article 8.

194. **The correct answer is (B) FALSE.** The sovereign rights over the continental shelf are exclusive — even if a state elects not to explore or develop resources within its continental shelf, no other state may exercise those rights.

195. **The correct answer is (C).** UNCLOS Articles 74 and 83 specify rules for delimiting overlapping claims to an EEZ and continental shelf between opposite and adjacent States. First States must attempt to resolve the dispute amicably. If States cannot reach a resolution, they are expected to enter into an interim agreement and to refer the dispute to the ICJ, which has resolved many such delimitation disputes. While there are some general rules with regard to how this delimitation typically occurs, there is no requirement that the

contested area be split equally or that one State yield entirely to the other. The timing of a State's declaration of an EEZ has no relevance to the ultimate boundaries that will be drawn. Therefore, **Answers (A), (D) and (E) are incorrect**. The common heritage of humanity refers to a plan for joint exploitation of manganese nodules on the deep seabed floor and has nothing to do with coastal zone delimitations. Therefore, **Answer (B) is also incorrect**.

196.   **The correct answer is (A).** UNCLOS Article 1(1) defines the area as the "seabed and ocean floor, and subsoils thereof, beyond the limits of national jurisdiction." UNCLOS Article 136 specifies that the Area is the common heritage of humanity, and under Article 140 is to be developed for the benefit of humanity as a whole. Article 152 establishes the International Seabed Authority to oversee exploitation of Area resources. **Answer (B) is incorrect** because exploitation and control over the continental shelf around Antarctica is governed by The 1991 Protocol on Environmental Protection to the Antarctic Treaty, which imposed a 50 year moratorium on mining and drilling for oil in the Antarctic Continental Shelf. **Answer (C) is incorrect** because the Area has nothing to do with the territorial sea. **Answer (D) is incorrect** because it refers to the so-called Bermuda Triangle. Although well-known in popular culture, there has never been any verification of the many paranormal claims associated with this region, which includes one of the most heavily traveled shipping lanes in the world. **Answer (E) is incorrect** because the Area has nothing to do with Arctic shipping routes.

197.   **The correct answer is (E).** Answers (A) and (B) are different ways of saying the same thing. Canada claims that the Northwest Passage, which separates the various islands of the Canadian Arctic Archipelago and the Canadian mainland are internal waters under Canadian Law (the Canadian Internal Waters Act) and under UNCLOS Article 46. This gives Canada the right to draw closing lines to delimit and define internal waters. **Answer (C) is incorrect** because UNCLOS Article 38 grants all ships and aircraft the right of transit passage through a strait. States opposed to Canada's claims over the Northwest Passage, including the United States, argue that the newly-exposed Arctic waters are an international strait rather than Canadian internal waters.

198.   **The correct answer is (A) TRUE.** Many of the provisions of UNCLOS confirmed customary law, and many other provisions of UNCLOS, like the 200 mile EEZ have rapidly become customary law. Even the United States, which historically refused to join UNCLOS over the Area's deep-sea bed mining provisions, considers the rest of the Convention to be customary law. With the Convention's near universal membership, and the acquiescence of non-member states like the United States, the practice of States has in nearly all respects been carried out in a manner consistent with the Convention, and those practices are considered mandatory under international law. As a result, it is fair to say that UNCLOS, which is widely accepted as the basis for all actions dealing with the oceans and the law of the sea, has become customary international law.

199.   **The correct answer is (C). Answer (A) is incorrect** because only coastal states can have EEZs. However, **Answers (B) and (D) are incorrect** because nothing in UNCLOS prohibits any state, landlocked or not, from fishing on the high seas. In fact, Article 87 specifically guarantees landlocked states the same rights in territorial waters, and EEZs as all other states, including the freedom to fish, and to conduct scientific research. Many states allow vessels of other states to fish in their EEZs, and Uganda would have just as much right

to participate on those terms as would any other state.

200. **The correct answer is (A) TRUE.** UNCLOS Article 20, requires that a submarine must navigate on the surface and must show its flag when transiting the territorial sea of another State. By contrast to innocent passage through territorial waters, UNCLOS Article 38 creates a right of transit passage through international straits. Transit passage does not place the same burdens of surfacing on submarines transiting international straits.

201. **The correct answer is (B) FALSE.** International Tribunal for the Law of the Sea has jurisdiction to interpret UNCLOS, but that jurisdiction is not exclusive. The dispute resolution mechanisms in Part XV of UNCLOS allow states quite a bit of flexibility. With the caveat in Article 279 that they commit to resolving their disputes peacefully, Article 280 specifies that states are free to choose whatever means they wish to resolve disputes arising under UNCLOS. UNCLOS's compulsory and binding procedures kick in only if states are unable to resolve their disputes on their own. Even for those compulsory procedures, states that are party to UNCLOS are free to select among the alternative dispute resolution methods and institutions provided for in Article 287 of UNCLOS. These alternatives include the Law of the Sea Tribunal, the ICJ, a general arbitral tribunal established persistent to Annex VII of UNCLOS or an arbitral tribunal composed of specialists in certain areas established pursuant to UNLCOS Annex VIII.

202. **The correct answer is (C).** UNCLOS Article 56(1)(a) does affirm that states have sovereign rights over living resources in their EEZs. However, Article 61(3) imposes an obligation to maintain living resources within the EEZ, and Article 63(1) calls on states to coordinate and agree on measures to ensure the conservation of fish stocks. Moreover, Articles 117-20 impose a duty on states to cooperate in the management and conservation of high seas living resources. Therefore, **Answer (A) is incorrect**. To flesh out these duties, the parties to UNCLOS negotiated an agreement governing conservation and management of straddling and migratory fish stocks (34 I.L.M. 1542). This agreement requires that states comply with, or create a regional fishing organization and agreement as a precondition of participating in a straddling stock fishery. UNCLOS gives no special obligations or status to "dominant states"; therefore **Answers (B) and (D) are incorrect**.

203. **The correct answer is (B) FALSE.** Along with the General Agreement on Trade in Services (GATS); the Agreement on Trade-Related Aspects of Intellectual Property Rights (TRIPS); and the Dispute Settlement Agreement, the GATT is one of the four key trade agreements administered by the WTO. It is true that the 1994 Marrakesh Agreement, which established the WTO, incorporated significant modifications to the pre-existing GATT agreement. But, the GATT remains a key agreement for managing international trade in goods.

204. **The correct answer is (A).** The Understanding on Settlement of Disputes, which is contained in Annex 2 of the WTO Agreement has a unique enforcement mechanism that gives the agreement more teeth than is usual for an international agreement. If a Dispute Settlement Panel rules against a party, that party can appeal the decision to the Appellate Body. The Appellate Body may uphold, modify or reverse the legal findings and conclusions of the panel. The Dispute Settlement Body (DSB) (which is composed of all of the member states) must then either adopt the report of the Appellate Body, or reject the report by consensus. If a party fails to comply with the recommendations and rulings within a reasonable time period, Article 3(7) and Article 22 of the Understanding allow the DSB to authorize countermeasures, or retaliatory action. The WTO does not have a police force, so **Answer (B) is incorrect.** Nor does it have a mandate to bring education to every school or to equitably share benefits. Therefore, **Answers (C) and (D) are incorrect.** Indeed, one of the main criticisms of the WTO is that states do not benefit equitably from the free trade regime it oversees, and in particular that developing countries are often on the losing end of free trade. The WTO has no special, streamlined negotiation procedures, so **Answer (E) is incorrect.**

205. **The correct answer is (C).** The WTO administers the GATT, the GATS, and TRIPS. **Answers (A) and (B) are incomplete and therefore incorrect.** There is no MIA agreement. In the mid-1990s, the OECD attempted to negotiate a multinational agreement on investing (MAI) that would have minimized the conditions that states could put on foreign investment. However, the effort was highly controversial because it was perceived as threatening the ability of states to regulate economic activity and protect the environment and worker safety. After a major public outcry, the OECD effort failed. Had the agreement been adopted, it would have been under the auspices of the OECD, not the WTO. Therefore, **Answer (D) is incorrect.** However, many states have bilateral investment agreements, and the WTO does administer a related agreement called the Trade Related Investment Measures which covers some aspects of foreign investment. And, the International Centre for Settlement on Investment Disputes (ICSID) provides a mechanism through which host countries, home countries and foreign investors can agree to submit investment disputes to third-Party arbitration.

206. **The correct answer is (B).** A key difference between the 1947 GATT and the 1995 GATT agreement is that a losing state can no longer block adoption of a dispute resolution ruling.

Prior to the Marrakesh Agreement, GATT dispute resolution decisions had to be adopted by consensus, which meant that a single objecting state (including the losing state) could block adoption of the ruling. **Answer (A) states the opposite and is therefore incorrect.** Now, under Article 16.4 of the DSU panel, decisions are automatically adopted unless there is a consensus to reject a ruling — any country wanting to block a ruling has to persuade all other WTO members (including its adversary in the case) to share its view. Although the GATT allows Bilateral Trade Agreements (BITs), neither version of the GATT required, prohibited or encouraged them. Therefore, **Answers (C), (D), and (E) are incorrect**.

207. **The correct answer is (B) FALSE.** The Dispute Settlement Body (DSB) does not hear arguments and resolve disputes under the WTO agreements. Instead, the DSB, which is comprised of representatives of all WTO members, is tasked with establishing Dispute Resolution Panels to review and decide such disputes, and with appointing the members of the WTO Appellate Body. It is these panels that sit in threes to hear arguments and resolve disputes. Although under Article 2.1 the DSB technically has sole authority to accept or reject recommended Dispute Resolution Panel and Appellate Body decisions, Article 16.4 of the Dispute Resolution Understanding (DSU), provides that Panel recommendations can only be rejected by consensus of the DSB. In addition to these tasks, the DSB is also responsible for monitoring the implementation of rulings and recommendations, and for authorizing countermeasures.

208. **The correct answer is (A).** Under Article 1.1 of the DSU, only member states can initiate dispute resolution proceedings. Article 3.2 of the DSU further emphasizes that the DSU exists to preserve the rights of Member States. Therefore, the other possible answers are incorrect. The Appellate Body has made it clear that there is no legal duty to accept briefs from anyone other than a WTO Member who is a party or third-party to the particular dispute. *United States — Imposition Of Countervailing Duties On Certain Hot-Rolled Lead And Bismouth Carbon Steel Products Originating In The United Kingdom*, WTO Doc. WT/DS138/AB/R of 10 May 2000. However, under DSU Article 13, a Panel may request information from any individual or body it deems appropriate. Thus, WTO panels can, and have, accepted amicus curiae briefs from NGOs.

209. **The correct answer is (B) FALSE.** Article 10.2 of the DSU explicitly permits any member state with a substantial interest in a matter before a panel to notify the DSB of its interest and to become a third party to the dispute. Third Parties have an opportunity to be heard by the panel and to make written submissions to the panel. Third Party submissions are also served on the parties, and the panel is expected to consider these submissions in its panel report.

210. **The correct answer is (B) FALSE.** After a panel recommendation is adopted by the DSB, a losing party has the option to appeal to the WTO Appellate Body. Only if there is no appeal does the case proceed directly to implementation of the panel decision.

211. **The correct answer is (D).** Article XI of the GATT reads in relevant part that parties shall establish "no prohibitions or restrictions" on the importation of any product that is permissible under the GATT. This provision prohibits most laws that impose trade barriers, even incidentally. Therefore, **Answers (A) and (C) are incorrect**. Article XX contains the permissible exceptions to Article XI. Article XX(g) of the GATT provides that: "Subject to the requirement that such measures are not applied in a manner which would constitute a

means of arbitrary or unjustifiable discrimination between countries where the same conditions prevail, or a disguised restriction on international trade, nothing in this Agreement shall be construed to prevent the adoption or enforcement by any contracting party of measures . . . relating to the conservation of exhaustible natural resources if such measures are made effective in conjunction with restrictions on domestic production or consumption." Therefore, **Answer (E) is incorrect**. However, the Appellate Body has interpreted this provision narrowly. The Shrimp-Turtle Decision found that a United States law banning import of tuna caught without a turtle excluder device fit within Article XX(g) but was still invalid because it was unduly discriminatory. As a result, Article XX provides limited protection for domestic environmental regimes, and **Answer (B) is incorrect**.

PRACTICE FINAL EXAM: ESSAY ANSWER

212. Before assessing the specifics of the conduct to which New Zealand is objecting, there are some preliminary questions that must be answered.

What is an Internationally Wrongful Act?

Under Article 2 of the Draft Articles on the Responsibility of States for Internationally Wrongful Acts, (Draft Articles) an internationally wrongful act is one that is: 1) attributable to a state; and 2) constitutes a breach of a state's obligation under international law. Although the Draft Articles have not yet been adopted as a treaty, they were cited by the ICJ in *Gabcikovo-Nagymaros*, and have been favorably received in general. It is an open question whether these Articles might be viewed as the distillation of a core of existing state practice or as a more proscriptive document intended to promote the progressive development of international law. This characterization matters for whether the Draft Articles will be viewed as a binding statement of customary law or a development of positive law that is binding only upon ratification. At a minimum, the Draft Articles are certainly some evidence of the relevant international standard for defining an internationally wrongful act

Under Article 13 of the Draft Articles, an act of a State does not constitute a breach of an international obligation unless the State is bound by the obligation in question at the time the act occurs. Thus while the Draft Articles set out the secondary rules of state responsibility, it is the ICRJH that defines the primary obligations in question. If the various allegations made by New Zealand in fact amount to violations of the ICRJH, these acts would probably qualify as internationally wrongful acts under the Draft Articles. Of course the specifics will vary for each state New Zealand is accusing (see below.)

Under Draft Articles 49-52, a state injured by an internationally wrongful act may have a right to take countermeasures if it demonstrates that the actions it is challenging are internationally wrongful acts. However, Article 55 indicates that these articles do not apply when there are special rules governing the question (or put another way, *lex specialis* trumps *lex generalis*). Article 37 of the ICRJH probably qualifies as such a special rule. Article 37 specifies that disputes are within the compulsory jurisdiction of the ICJ. Therefore, New Zealand might be prohibited from taking unilateral countermeasures rather than pursuing its rights before the ICJ. If New Zealand does wind up taking countermeasures, such measures must be proportional to the injury suffered. (Art. 51)

Does New Zealand have standing to raise a complaint about these putatively internationally wrongful Acts?

Under Article 42 of the Draft Articles, there are two pre-conditions before a state may be considered injured for the purposes of invoking the responsibility of another state. First, the obligation breached must be owed 1) to that state individually; 2) to a group of states including that state; or 3) to the international community as a whole. Second, the breach of the obligation must either specifically affect the complaining state or be of such a character that it radically changes the position of all other States to which the obligation is owed.

In this situation, the relevant primary obligation would be the ban on Jabberwocky hunting in Article 11 of the ICRJH. New Zealand would have to show that the states it is challenging owed it the obligation to not hunt Jabberwocky and that New Zealand has been injured by the breach of this obligation. The language in Article 31 of the ICRJH specifying that any party may bring a proceeding before the ICJ lends support to New Zealand's claim of injury.

Another potentially relevant primary obligation might be the CITES Art. 2 restrictions on trade in species listed in CITES Appendix 1. Depending on the circumstances, New Zealand might make a claim that the conduct of some or all of these states is in violation of international restrictions on trade in endangered species. However, the facts do not provide enough information to decide whether such a claim would be viable. The terms of dispute resolution in CITES Art. 18 are permissive rather than mandatory and therefore do not raise the same *lex specialis* concerns as the ICRJH.

Analysis of the Specific Allegations

Assuming that New Zealand has standing, the question then becomes whether the conduct of each state amounts to an internationally wrongful act. The analysis for each state will be dealt with sequentially below.

1. Legality of Canadian Jabberwoky hunting

Canada is a party to the ICRJH. Canada made a reservation when it signed the ICRJH allowing it to authorize aboriginal groups to take up to 10 Jabberwocky per year. The key question will be whether Canada's reservation validly amends its obligations under the ICRJH and exempts its conduct from the Article 11 moratorium. If so, then Canada has not breached an international obligation and therefore cannot be said to have committed an internationally wrongful act.

What is the effect of Canada's Reservation?

Article 19 of the Vienna Convention on the Law of Treaties (Vienna Convention) allows a state to make a reservation to a treaty it joins so long as the reservation does not undermine the objective and purpose of the treaty. (Vienna Convention Art. 19(c)). In this case Canada's reservation is a significant but still fairly small deviation from the absolute ban. If the purpose of the ban is to restore Jabberwocky stocks to sustainable levels, then Canada's small hunting exception probably does not undermine the objective and purpose of the treaty. If the treaty instead seeks to ban Jabberwocky hunting because that hunt is deemed absolutely immoral or illegal, than any deviation would undermine the purpose of the treaty. While a cultural agreement has grown up about the immorality of Jabberwocky hunting since the ban was imposed, that subsequent development does not change the purpose of the treaty. Moreover, in light of the facts that the Article 11 ban is not permanent; that the treaty contemplates reevaluating the ban based on scientific criteria, and that the ICRJH already contemplates some continued Jabberwocky hunting under Article 14, it seems likely that Canada's exception does not undermine the treaty.

The fact that the exception focuses on indigenous rights further underscores its validity. Indigenous rights have become an area of increasing concern in international law. Article 11 of the Declaration on Indigenous Rights, adopted by the General Assembly in 2007, affirms that indigenous people have a right to practice their cultural traditions and customs. Article

20 emphasizes that indigenous people have a right to engage in traditional activities and a right to subsistence. Although the Declaration is not binding law, it represents a significant recognition that international law must be interpreted in a fashion that does not compromise the rights of indigenous people. Because Canada's exception to the ICRJH is in furtherance of a basic right of indigenous peoples, it is likely to be interpreted as a legitimate reservation rather than one undermining the core purpose of the treaty.

Under Article 20(5) of the Vienna Convention, a party may object to a reservation within one year of being notified of the reservation. New Zealand explicitly rejected the reservation within one year of Canada's action. Under Article 21(3) the effect of New Zealand's rejection of Canada's reservation is that the treaty enters into force but the reserved-portion has no effect between the relevant states. Thus the Article 11 ban is not in force between New Zealand and Canada.

Under the circumstances, New Zealand will not be able to demonstrate that Canada has breached an international obligation that it owes New Zealand.

2. Legality of Japanese Jabberwocky hunting

Japan is a late-comer to the treaty, joining in 1986. Upon joining, it lodged a unilateral instrument purporting to limit its obligations under the treaty (the instrument may be considered to be an exception) and to allow continued extensive jabberwocky hunting. If the instrument is a valid exception, Japan's activities would not be a violation of the agreement. Unlike Canada's exception, New Zealand did not object to Japan's unilateral instrument. However, an exception cannot change the terms of the ICRJH or the side-agreement already in existence. To the extent that this instrument purports to allow continued extensive jabberwocky hunting under the guise of research, it directly contradicts the purpose and intent of the agreement. Under Vienna Convention Art. 18, signatories to a treaty have an ancillary duty to "refrain from acts which would defeat the object and purpose of the treaty."

Even if Japan's instrument is a valid statement of the obligations Japan owes to subsequent joiners, who joined the treaty subject to Japan's instrument, it cannot retroactively limit the obligations that Japan owes New Zealand, a pre-existing party to the agreement. (Vienna Convention Article 40(4)) So, either the instrument means that Japan did not in fact join the treaty or it is invalid with regard to New Zealand and cannot limit the obligations Japan owes New Zealand. It seems that the more likely outcome, given that Japan has participated in the treaty regime for almost two decades and clearly considers itself a party (as evidenced by its participation in the Southern Sanctuary vote) the more likely outcome is that the exception is invalid.

Japans will also assert that its jabberwocky hunting activities fits within the Article 14 scientific research exception. If so, then Japan's activities fit within the scope of the ICRJH. Thus Japan would not have breached an international obligation and therefore could be said to have committed an internationally wrongful act.

To answer this question, we must interpret the scientific research exception. Articles 31 and 32 of the Vienna Convention specify that treaty terms must be given their good faith, ordinary meaning, as derived from the context and in light of the treaty's object and purpose. Examining Japan's conduct under that standard, it seems likely that Japan has violated its obligations under Article 11.

Under Vienna Convention Article 31(2)(a), "context" includes the preamble as well as any agreement relating to the treaty which was made between all parties in connection with the conclusion of the treaty. In this case, there was a contemporaneous supplementary agreement to the ICRJH, adopted by all parties to the agreement that defined "scientific research" to mean a very limited number of catches. This definition of scientific research also prohibited the sale for consumption of any jabberwockies caught for research.

Even if Japan did not join the side agreement when it joined the ICRJH and is not directly bound by the agreement (and the unilateral declaration makes it seem like Japan probably did not join) the side agreement is still relevant for interpreting the meaning of terms in the ICRJH because under the Vienna Convention, "context" for purposes of interpreting the Article 14 ICRJH scientific research exception includes this supplementary agreement. This obviously cuts against Japan's argument and in favor of New Zealand's because Japan's activities do not fit within this definition of scientific research. The scale of Japan's activities is much greater than the very limited activities contemplated by the ICRJH side agreement. Moreover, the side agreement explicitly prohibits selling the byproducts of scientific research for consumption. The fact that Japan's domestic laws authorize conduct contrary to the ban on selling byproducts for consumption is not a defense to an otherwise internationally wrongful act. Draft Articles 32, entitled "Irrelevance of Internal Law" specifically provides that a state may not rely on the provisions of its internal law as justification for failure to comply with its international obligations.

Context would also include the statements in the ICRJH Preamble that arguably signal that the purpose of the treaty is to restore Jabberwocky populations in order to continue exploiting them. While this does not directly support Japan, it undercuts any attempt by New Zealand to take an absolute preservationist stand on the treaty, and may bring the treaty into potential conflict with CITES.

In addition to the context described above, Art. 31(3)(b) of the Vienna Convention states that in addition to context, treaty interpretation should also take into account subsequent interpretive agreements and subsequent practice shedding light on that interpretation. Even if Japan's 1986 unilateral instrument were considered a subsequent interpretive agreement because the twenty states joining the ICRJH after Japan have affirmed Japan's unilateral agreement, this argument would be very weak. First, no state other than Japan has caught whales in excess of the quantity specified in the side agreement. Thus, actual practice of the treaty members indicates adherence to this provision as the law governing their conduct. Moreover, the ICRJH decision to found the Southern Sanctuary cuts against such an argument, because it indicates a continuing intent to protect Jabberwockies from hunting in the name of science.

Japan will also argue that the preparatory materials for the ICRJH indicate that there was no intent to really create a 100 year moratorium. However, under Article 32 of the Vienna Convention, preparatory materials are only relevant to treaty interpretation when they confirm an interpretation reached through context, or when context either leaves a treaty term ambiguous or leads to an absurd interpretation. Japan will have to argue absurdity here.

If the preparatory materials are considered, they might support Japan's broad interpretation of the scientific exception because at least some of the materials indicate an assumption that the scientific exception will be interpreted broadly. However, attempts to change the language of the ICRJH to reflect the understanding expressed in the preparatory materials failed, so it is not clear how much mileage Japan will really get out of this material.

There is also some support for the position that a 100 year moratorium is absurd in recent writings of eminent jurists like Professor Wolfrum. However, should this dispute get to the ICJ, writings of eminent jurists contradicting an express term in the ICRJH would not be considered dispositive. Under the ICJ statute, writings of jurists are a subsidiary source of international law (ICJ Statute Art. 38(d)) and are unlikely to be definitive in the wake of an explicit treaty provision (Art. 38(a)). However, in its *Fukyshima Advisory Opinion*, the ICJ recently indicated some flexibility in interpreting very long moratoria. That decision is not binding on New Zealand, both because ICJ Article 59 limits the effect of ICJ decisions to the parties and because the prior decision was an advisory opinion not a contentious case. Nevertheless, it offers some indication of how the ICJ might approach such a question. In *Fukyshima* the ICJ emphasized that reading a lengthy moratorium too strictly, particularly if it impinged on deep-seated cultural practices, might be an impermissible burden on state sovereignty. Were the court to approach the question of Japan's conduct through this lens, it might well conclude that interpreting the 100 year moratorium literally would be absurd Were it to do so, it might then draw from Professor Wolfrum to support its decision.

Regardless of whether Japan's activities fit within the scientific exception, it is clear that Japan's activities in the Southern Sanctuary are illegal. The members of the ICRJH voted in 1994 to declare the oceans around Antarctica to be a Jabberwocky sanctuary. Although Japan voted against this decision, it did not file an exception to the decision. As a member of the ICRJH, Japan is therefore bound by the designation of the Southern Sanctuary. Its hunting activities have violated this part of the ICRJH agreement.

3. Legality of Argentinean Jabberwocky hunting

Under Article 13 of the Draft Articles, an act of a State does not constitute a breach of an international obligation unless the State is bound by the obligation in question at the time the act occurs. Argentina has only signed but not ratified the ICRJH.

Under Vienna Convention Art 26, a treaty binds only the parties (pacta sunt servanda). However, under Vienna Convention Art. 18, signatories have an ancillary duty to "refrain from acts which would defeat the object and purpose of the treaty."

In this case, Argentina's actions in catching hundreds of Jabberwocky significantly exceed the scope of the scientific exception to the Jabberwocky hunting moratorium. If Argentina is bound by the moratorium, it is in violation of its obligations under international law. Even if Argentina is not bound by the moratorium, it may have violated international law if its actions jeopardize the purpose of the ICRJH.

The question is what obligations Argentina has under these circumstances. By signing the treaty, Argentina has invoked its duty under Article 18 of the Vienna Convention. The issue of the scope of duties under these circumstances has come up with regard to the United States attempts to undermine the International Criminal Court, particularly by enacting domestic legislation authorizing an invasion of the Hague if necessary to prevent the ICC from exercising jurisdiction over US citizens, and by pressuring states to sign bilateral agreements with the United States that ensure that US citizens will not be turned over to the ICC. The United States signed the Rome Treaty, but has never ratified it. Numerous eminent jurists have written about the United States duties under this circumstance. The general consensus seems to be that the United States has no obligation to comply with the terms of the Rome Treaty but cannot lawfully work to defeat the aims of the treaty. Subject to the caveats described above, those writings might be relevant to an interpretation of Argentina's duties.

Argentina's actions are certainly not on the scale of the US with regard to the ICC. Argentina is not pressuring parties to the ICRJH to violate their commitments under that agreement. It seems like the only way that Argentina could be construed to be acting to undermine the ICRJH is if the state of Jabberwocky populations is in fact extremely precarious. If so, Argentina's actions in hunting Jabberwocky might defeat the object and purpose of the ICRJH which is to stabilize and preserve Jabberwocky populations for future generations. Otherwise, it is hard to see how Argentina's actions violate international law.

4. Legality of Icelandic Jabberwocky hunting

Iceland is not a member of the ICRJH. Under Article 13 of the Draft Articles, an act of a State does not constitute a breach of an international obligation unless the State is bound by the obligation in question at the time the act occurs. Under Art. 34 of the Vienna convention, a treaty cannot create obligations for a non-party without the consent of the non-party. Under Article 35 of the Vienna Convention, a treaty creates obligations for third parties only when the parties to the treaty intend to create third party obligations and the third party expressly accepts that obligation in writing. That did not happen here. So, the ICRJH itself cannot be a source of obligations for Iceland.

The only way that Iceland's activities can be unlawful under international law is if the moratorium can be characterized as a customary rule of international law. Customary law applies to all states by virtue of their existence as states and does not hinge on an express affirmation of the duty on the part the state. So, if the moratorium, which is an obligation created by treaty, has become customary law, it will apply equally to all states, including those not party to the treaty.

Under Art. 38(1)(b) of the ICJ statute, a rule is customary international law when it reflects a general practice that is accepted as a legal obligation. Thus two elements must be present for the moratorium to be considered customary law: 1) there must be a general practice by States abiding by the moratorium over a long period of time, and there must be the generally-held belief that this practice is required by law.

New Zealand will have a hard time demonstrating that the moratorium has become customary law given that Japan and Argentina in addition to Iceland are acting contrary to the moratorium. (Canada's actions are arguably consistent with the moratorium so are not evidence that the moratorium is not general practice.)

The mere fact that Iceland's actions are contrary to New Zealand law does not make those actions a violation of international law (the same is true of Canada, Japan and Argentina.)

INDEX

INDEX